A Whistle in the Dark

D1584642

Methuen Drama

5 7 9 10 8 6 4

First published in 1970 by The Gallery Press, Dublin
Reprinted, with revisions, in *Tom Murphy Plays: 4* in 1989
by Methuen Drama

This edition published in 2001 by
Methuen Drama
A & C Black Publishers Limited
36 Soho Square
London W1D 3QY
www.methuendrama.com

A CIP catalogue record for this book is available
from the British Library

ISBN 978 0 413 61500 8

Typeset by Wilmaset Ltd, Birkenhead, Wirral
Printed and bound in Great Britain by
CPI Cox & Wyman, Reading, Berkshire

A Whistle in the Dark

by Tom Murphy

Methuen Drama

This edition of **A Whistle in the Dark** has been re-published
to coincide with the Abbey and Peacock Theatre's major season
of plays by Tom Murphy held in October 2001.

The National Theatre gratefully acknowledges the financial
support from the Arts Council/An Chomhairle Ealaíon

A Whistle in the Dark

by Tom Murphy

A Whistle in the Dark by Tom Murphy opened at the Abbey Theatre on 2 October, 2001.

The play is set in Coventry in 1961.

Cast

Michael Carney	Declan Conlon
Harry Carney	Don Wycherley
Des Carney	Barry Ward
Iggy Carney	David Herlihy
Hugo Carney	Gary Lydon
Dada	Clive Geraghty
Betty	Cathy Belton
Mush	Phelim Drew
Director	Conall Morrison
Set Designer	Tim Reed
Costume Designer	Joan O'Clery
Lighting Designer	Rupert Murray
Sound	Dave Nolan
Stage Director	Audrey Hession
Assistant Stage Manager	Marella Boschi
Voice Coach	Andrea Ainsworth
Festival Producer	Una Carmody
Set	Abbey Theatre Workshop
Costumes	Abbey Theatre Wardrobe Department

Tom Murphy

Plays include:

On the Outside *(w. Noel O'Donoghue)*
A Whistle in the Dark
The Orphans
A Crucial Week in the Life of a Grocer's Assistant
Famine
The Morning After Optimism
The White House
On the Inside
The Sanctuary Lamp
The J. Arthur Maginnis Story
Epitaph Under Ether *(a compilation from the works of J.M.Synge)*
The Blue Macushla
The Informer *(from the novel by Liam O'Flaherty)*
Conversations on a Homecoming
The Gigli Concert
Bailegangaire
A Thief of a Christmas
Too Late for Logic
The Patriot Game
Cupa Coffee
She Stoops to Folly *(from The Vicar of Wakefield)*
The Wake
The House

And a novel, **The Seduction of Morality**

He has received numerous awards and nominations.
Awards include: Irish Academy of Letters Award, Harveys Irish Theatre Award (twice), Sunday Tribune Arts Award, Independent Newspapers Theatre Award, Sunday Independent/Irish Life Award, Drama-Logue Critics Award, Irish Times/ESB Lifetime Award, Irish Times/ESB Theatre Award (Best Play) and Honorary Degrees from University of Dublin (Trinity College) and NUI (Galway). He was born in Tuam, County Galway. He lives in Dublin.

Conall Morrison *Director*

Conall is an Associate Director of the National Theatre where productions on the Abbey stage include his own adaptation of Patrick Kavanagh's **Tarry Flynn,** (also a Lyttleton Theatre, Royal National Theatre), Boucicault's **The Colleen Bawn** (also Lyttleton Theatre), Brian Friel's **The Freedom of the City, The Tempest** and Tom Murphy's **The House** and at the Peacock Gary Mitchell's **In a Little World of Our Own** and **As the Beast Sleeps** and **Twenty Grand** by Declan Hughes. Other productions include **Conquest of the South Pole, The Marlboro Man, Emma, Measure for Measure, Dancing at Lughnasa, Juno and the Paycock, Macbeth, Kvetch, Martin Guerre** for Cameron Mackintosh at the West Yorkshire Playhouse and at the Guthrie Centre Minneapolis. His own plays include **Rough Justice, Green, Orange and Pink** and **Hard to Believe**. He has won an Irish Times/ESB Best Director Award and a Sunday Independent/Spirit of Life Award.

Joan O'Clery *Costume Designer*

Joan's work at the Abbey and Peacock Theatres includes **Blackwater Angel, The House, The Tempest, The Wake** which toured to the Edinburgh Festival, **The Freedom of the City,** which toured to the Lincoln Center, New York and **The Colleen Bawn** which toured to the Royal National Theatre, London, **Kevin's Bed, Give Me Your Answer, Do!, A Woman of No Importance, Macbeth, The Only True History of Lizzie Finn, Philadelphia, Here I Come!, Observe the Sons of Ulster Marching Towards the Somme, Sive, The Last Apache Reunion, Rumpelstiltskin, The Third Law of Motion, Something's in the Way** and **Toupees and Snaredrums,** a CoisCéim/Abbey Theatre co-production. Joan designed the costumes for the Gate Theatre's production of **Oleanna** and was the winner of the 1997 Irish Times/ESB Costume Designer of the Year Award for her work on the Gate Theatre's **Pinter Festival**. Last year she designed the costumes for **Peer Gynt** at the Royal National Theatre, London. She also designed **Sive** by John B. Keane, Palace Theatre, Watford and Tricycle, **Licking the Marmalade Spoon,** Project Arts Centre and **Judith** at project @ the mint.

Tim Reed *Designer*

Tim's work at the Abbey and Peacock Theatres includes **The Beaux' Stratagem**, **The Field**, **Exit**, **Entrance** and **The Shadow of a Gunman**. Other theatre work includes **Happy Days**, **The House of Bernarda Alba**, Gate Theatre, **Curtains**, Hampstead and Whitehall Theatres, Frank McGuinness's **Bag Lady**, Traverse Theatre, Edinburgh, Anthony Minghella's **Two Planks and a Passion**, Northcott Theatre, Exeter, **Hobson's Choice** and **Spring and Port Wine** at the West Yorkshire Playhouse. Opera credits include **Don Giovanni** with Clare Venables, Gothenberg **Doktor Faustus**, **L'Ormindo**, Netherlands Opera, **Macbeth**, Madrid, **La Traviata** and **The Turn of the Screw**, Israel, and **Cosi Fan Tutte**, Dublin, **Der Rosenkavalier**, **Die Fledermaus** and **La Traviata**, **L'Elisir D'Amore**, Gothenberg Opera, **The Coronation of Poppea** and **The Marriage of Figaro** for Norrlands Opera, UMEA, **Cendrillon** and **La Vedova Scaltra**, Wexford Festival, **Albert Herring** for Opera '80 and for Opera Northern Ireland **Cunning Little Vixen**, **Macbeth**, **Falstaff**, **Ariadne auf Naxos** and **Le nozze di Figaro** also for Kirov Opera in St Petersburg. Tim has had five exhibitions of painting. Future engagements include two new exhibitions of work in the spring and a production of Georges Fedeaux' **Horse and Carriage** at the West Yorkshire Playhouse.

Rupert Murray *Lighting Designer*

Rupert is a freelance lighting designer and producer. Recent lighting designs include Jim Nolan's **Blackwater Angel**, Brian Friel's **Translations**, Abbey Theatre, Shelagh Stephenson's **The Memory of Water** for the Peacock Theatre, Neil LaBute's **Bash** and Noel Coward's **Blithe Spirit** at the Gate Theatre, as well as their touring productions of Samuel Beckett's **I'll Go On**, **Waiting for Godot** and **Krapp's Last Tape**. He is the lighting designer for **Riverdance - The Show** which is currently touring the USA and Europe. Rupert was Festival Director of the St Patrick's Festival from 1995 to 1999 and was a key member of the team which transformed Ireland's national celebrations. He has also been responsible for staging and directing the opening and closing festivities at the Wexford Festival Opera for the last three years. Through his company *Creative Events* he produces and stages major corporate, civic and theatrical events all around Ireland.

The Abbey Theatre would like to thank:

Sponsors
Aer Lingus
Anglo Irish Bank
Calouste Gubenkian Foundation
Ferndale Films
Dr. A. J. F. O'Reilly
Oman Moving & Storage
RTE
Smurfit Ireland Ltd
Viacom Outdoor
The Irish Times

Benefactors
Aer Rianta
AIB Group
An Post
Behaviour and Attitudes
eircom
Electricity Supply Board
Independent News and Media PLC
Irish Life & Permanent plc
IIB Bank
Merc Partners
John & Viola O'Connor
Pfizer International Bank Europe
Scottish Provident Ireland
SDS
SIPTU
Unilever Ireland plc
VHI

Patrons
J. G. Corry
Brian Friel
Guinness Ireland Group
Irish Actors Equity
Gerard Kelly & Co
McCullough-Mulvin Architects
Mercer Ltd
Smurfit Corrugated Cases
Sumitomo Finance (Dublin)
Total Print and Design
Francis Wintle

Sponsors of the
National Theatre Archive
Jane & James O'Donoghue
Sarah & Michael O'Reilly
Rachel & Victor Treacy

Friends of the Abbey
Patricia Barnett
Mr. Ron Bolger
Ms. Patricia Brown
Ms. Ann Byrne
Mr. Joseph Byrne
Ms. Zita Byrne
Lilian & Robert Chambers
Ms. Orla Cleary
Claire Cronin
Ms. Dolores Deacon
Ms. Patricia Devlin
Karen Doull
Paul & Florence Flynn
Ms. Christina Goldrick
Mrs. Rosaleen Hardiman
Sean & Mary Holahan
Mrs. Madeleine Humphreys
Ms. Eileen Jackson
Ms. Kate Kavanagh
Mr. Francis Keenan
Mr. Peter Keenan
Vivienne & Kieran Kelly
Joan & Michael Keogh
Donal & Máire Lowry
Mr. Fechin Maher
Una M. Moran
McCann FitzGerald Solicitors
Ellie McCullough
Mr. Joseph McCullough
Marcella & Aidan McDonnell
Liam MacNamara
Dr. Chris Morash
Mr. Frank Murray
Mr. Vincent O'Doherty
Ms. Mary O'Driscoll
Mr. Dermot & Ita O'Sullivan
Mr. Andrew Parkes
Mr. Terry Patmore
Dr. Colette Pegum
Mr. Michael P. Quinn
Mr. Noel Ryan
Breda & Brendan Shortall
Fr. Frank Stafford

Personnel

A Whistle in the Dark

A Whistle in the Dark was first performed at the Theatre Royal, Stratford East, in 1961 with the following cast:

Michael Carney	Michael Craig
Harry Carney	Darren Nesbit
Des Carney	Dudley Sutton
Iggy Carney	Oliver McGreery
Hugo Carney	James Mellor
Dada	Patrick Magee
Betty	Dorothy Bromley
Mush	Seán Lynch

Act One

The play opens on a confusion of noise, movement and preparation. The room and its effects show signs of misuse. There are three doors: one opens to the hall, front door and front room, the second to the kitchen and rear of house, the third to the stairs. **Harry,** *in vest and trousers, barefooted, carrying his shoes and one sock, is looking for the other sock. He is about thirty.* **Hugo** *comes rushing downstairs to go to the mirror and give a liberal dressing of oil to his hair; he is singing snatches of a pop song which appears to hold a personal amusement for him; he is rather stupid.* **Iggy** *is fully dressed, waiting impatiently. He is a big man, the biggest in the family, and fancies his image in his good suit. He stammers occasionally – in moments of tension. He affects a swagger when he walks; the swagger is called 'the gimp': shoulders hunched up, one shoulder higher than the other, arms slightly tensed and held out a little from the sides, and thumbs sticking outwards from the sides. This is the walk of 'a tough-un', an 'iron man'. Fighting is an innate part of* **Iggy***'s character and is not without a touch of nobility in his case.* **Betty** *is English, about twenty-eight. She enters and exits through the scene, with bedclothes, pillows, etc., to and from the front room.*

Generally, all of them are preoccupied with themselves.

Harry (*looking for sock*)   Sock-sock-sock-sock-sock? Hah? Where is it? Sockeen–sockeen–sockeen?

Hugo (*singing*)   'Here we go loopey loop, here we go loopey laa . . .'

Harry   Now–now–now, sock–sock!

Betty   Do you want me to see if that camp-bed is going to be too short for you, Iggy?

Harry (*without looking at her, pokes a finger in her ribs as she passes by*)   Greeks! (*Continues search for sock.*) Hah? Sockeen.

Betty   Iggy?

Iggy   Are we r-r-ready?

Harry (*in frustration*)   Stock-king!

Hugo   Maybe you dropped it on the stairs.

Iggy *dashes up the stairs. The doorbell is ringing.* **Betty** *going to answer it.* **Hugo** *beats her to it and admits* **Mush**. **Hugo** *and* **Mush** *in front hall, in greeting to each other, singing 'Here we go loopey loop . . .'*

Harry (*simultaneously, finding missing sock in one of his shoes*)   Aaa! Hidey-hidey, was you? (*Drops his shoes with a clatter on the floor.*)

Hugo *and* **Mush** *entering.* **Mush** *is about thirty, a small fella, cheapish new suit; sycophantic.*

Mush   'Allo-'allo-'allo!

Harry (*sniffing socks*)   These has been dead for a year or more.

Hugo   Did you find it?

Mush   I wasn't long, was I?

Harry *throws his balled-up socks at* **Mush***;* **Mush** *catches them and throws them at* **Hugo***;* **Hugo** *retaliates by throwing a cup at* **Mush** *which smashes against the wall,* **Mush** *shooting at it with an imaginary gun.* **Betty** *exits to kitchen.*

Harry   Easy with the delph –

Iggy (*entering with* **Harry***'s shirt which he dumps on a chair*) Sh-sh-shirt. Sh-sh-shirt –

Harry   Jesus, d'yeh want me to cut the feet of myself! (*He has picked his way across the room to search in a drawer for a clean pair of socks.*)

Mush   Heigh-up, Ig!

Iggy   T-t-t-train'll be in.

Harry (*finds clean pair of socks*)   Doesn't this colour suit our Michael now? Boghole brown.

Iggy   Harry, t-t-t-train.

Harry (*there is a hole in one of the socks*)   Jesus! Person'lly, my 'pinion, English women is no good, 'cept for maybe readin' real true love stories. (*Calls to kitchen where* **Betty** *is.*) Oi! No use English birds.

Iggy   We-we-we ready?

Harry   No value for money is English flesh.

Iggy (*to* **Hugo**)   Look at the t-t-time.

Hugo   Better run all right. Be (*a*) nice thing for Dada and Des to arrive and we not there.

Harry   Don't mind selling but person'lly wouldn't be wasting good money on no English charver. Oi, Mush?

Mush (*picking up pieces of broken crockery*)   England, beauty and home, Har.

Iggy *sighs heavily over* **Harry**'s *perverse slow dressing and is unconsciously thumping the door-panel behind him.*

Hugo   Ever seen a man put his fist through a door?

Mush   I seen a fella one night –

Iggy   E-e-ever s-s-seen a man open a door without turning the knob?

Hugo *nods in invitation to* **Iggy** *to try it.* **Michael** *is heard coming in front door.*

Hugo   Stall it: Michael.

Harry   Hold on to it. (*The door knob.*)

Iggy *is holding the handle against* **Michael** *who is on the other side of the door.* **Hugo** *is giggling.*

Michael   Betty!

Harry   Is he trying against you? (**Iggy** *nods.*) . . . Now! Let it go.

Iggy *releases the door handle: the expected (***Michael** *to come flying in) does not happen. After a moment* **Michael** *enters. He is* *in his working clothes – perhaps a boiler-suit which he gets out of during the following scene. He is about thirty-five.*

Harry   Our Michael would've made a great footballer: that's what's called antic'pation.

Michael   That train will be in now.

Iggy, **Mush** *and* **Hugo** *exit –* **Hugo** *singing 'Here we go loopey loop'.*

Harry *putting on his jacket is having some difficulty with the lining in the sleeve, but containing his irritation.*

Harry   Not coming with us to meet Dada and Des?

Michael   I'll get the beds and things fixed up.

Iggy (*off*)   H-h-harry!

Harry   The beds and things are fixed up. (*Still smiling but thrusts his fist and arm viciously through the sleeve of his jacket.*) Hah?

He follows the others out.

Michael (*calls to kitchen*)   Heigh-up!

Betty *comes in and starts to tidy up in silence.*

Michael   . . . Your slip is – (*Showing.*)

Betty   It's clean.

He shuts the front door and returns with a paper bag containing some bottles of beer which he has left in the hall. They look at each other for a moment. Then she smiles at him and shakes her head to herself.

Betty (*referring to his brothers*)   Honestly!

Michael   I got a few bottles of beer. Keep them happy.

Betty   I still think you should have gone to the station.

Michael   There's enough of a reception committee gone down. They'll be here in a few minutes.

Betty   Things are going to be cramped.

Michael   It'll be just for a week anyway.

Betty   Maybe Des would stay on.

Michael   No. Just a holiday.

Betty   Will your father mind sharing a room?

Michael   Are the beds fixed up okay?

Betty   Will your father – Well, will he like me, sort of?

Michael   Come here to me, Brummy.

Betty   The house is really awful. I can't help it.

Michael   No, you'll like Des.

Betty   I've heard enough about him anyway. When you proposed I thought you'd say, Des and I would like you to marry me – you – us – whatever it is.

Michael   No, you'll like him. He's not like me – I think you'll like him.

Betty   There will be seven of us for tea. There's only four cups in the house now.

Michael   They all won't want tea.

Betty   I've eight saucers.

Michael   You can buy some tomorrow. Just Dada and Des.

Betty   That's all right, but this buying more cups business, and putting in more panes of glass, and –

Michael   Not tonight.

Betty   What? But isn't it daft? Everything. Look. Just look at the place after a few weeks of family life with your brothers. And now two more.

Michael   Not tonight, Josephine.

Betty   You what?

Michael (*English accent, joking*) You what? We can drink out of the saucers; it's an old Irish custom.

Betty No, it's daft.

Michael And we'll get a little pig, a bonham, to run around the kitchen as a house pet.

Betty Daft.

Michael And we'll be progressive, and grow shamrocks instead of geraniums. And turn that little shed at the end of the garden into a hotel for the fairies and leprechauns.

Betty You're daft. You really are. We were doing pretty well before you asked them here. Daft!

Michael And we'll –

Betty (*suddenly serious*) No, I don't think it's small or funny.

Michael Neither do I.

Betty I'm not saying your father and Des aren't welcome, but the others –

Michael Not tonight.

Betty It's all right trying to be the big brother but you're not getting on so well with them, are you?

Michael Not tonight.

Betty Well, when are you going to –

Michael This isn't the time anyway!

Betty I think it's as good a time as any.

Michael Oh, leave it so, can't you! You're rushing around like mad. Have a rest for a while or something. The place is fine.

Betty What?

Michael The place is fine! Relax, have a rest, I'll give you a shout when they come.

Betty   Upstairs, is it? That is, if the fighting and crashing all over the place doesn't start. Is it the table or chairs that got it this time?

Michael   Yes – yes – yes.

Betty   Who will make the bid to sleep with me tonight?

Michael   Don't make a big thing out of it. Harry was drunk that night.

Betty   Harry is drunk tonight, the others are drunk, they're always drunk.

Michael   Don't start, for Christ's sake! Jesus, haven't I enough on my mind!

Betty   All right. Quiet so. But look at it this way: I married you, not your brothers. Since you asked them here we've hardly gone near each other. If I'm on my own here, I'm standing in there (*kitchen*) afraid to make a sound; if I'm upstairs I'm afraid to make a sound. That's just natural, is it?

Michael   Look –

Betty   That's the way every young married couple is, is it?

Michael   They're a bit wild –

Betty   Wild? Hah!

Michael   Yes! Wild! A bit wild. They're my brothers, I have a responsibility. It's our family. A bit wild. They never got a chance. They'll change.

Betty   You're going to bring that about?

Michael   I'm the eldest –

Betty   Your father is the eldest. What about your responsibility to me? You're married now, you know.

Michael   I know.

Betty   (*silently*)   I see.

Michael   Look –

Betty   Which comes first, which is more important to you, me or your brothers?

Michael   That's silly, stupid talk.

Betty   Is it? It usen't be.

Michael   Look, what do you think will happen –

Betty   What do you think will happen to me!

Michael   And with Des coming here now –

Betty   To hell with Des and the rest of them! It's us or them. Which is more important to you?

Michael *goes out to the hall, opens front door and stands outside for a few moments. He returns to the room.*

Michael   Harry and Mush are coming with the cases. (*He puts his arm round* **Betty**.)

Betty   Maybe you should ask Mush to move in with us too.

Michael   Shh, Brummy. Your slip is still showing.

Betty   I don't know.

Michael   It'll be okay.

Betty *goes into the kitchen.* **Harry** *and* **Mush** *enter.*

Mush   Niggers?

Harry   No.

Mush   Blacks?

Harry   No, I wouldn't call them that neither.

Michael   Did they arrive all right?

Mush   Muslims?

Harry (*considers this*)   Yeh. That's fair. We're Catholics. I got the first good beltin' I got for years off the Muslims a few weeks ago. (*To* **Michael**.) Hah?

Michael   Did they arrive okay?

Harry   But I still like them. Respect them. Blacks, Muslims. They stick together, their families and all. And if they weren't here, like, our Irish blue blood would turn a shade darker, wouldn't it? (*To* **Michael**.) Hah? And then some people'd want our cocks chopped off too.

Mush   One-way tickets back to the jungle for us too, Har, if they weren't here.

Michael   Are they coming?

Harry   Hah? Dada is looking great, you'll love to hear, Michael.

Mush   The lousers must have stayed on for another one at The Lion.

Harry   Des too.

Mush   He's a Carney all right.

Harry   Yeh. He's got big, big, bones, loose, he'll be a hard hitter.

Mush   When he learns about the nut.

Harry (*laughs*)   He's learned it. His first lesson, Michael. Half an hour over and young Des has a scrap already.

Michael   What? What happened?

Harry   Aw! You're awful worried, aren't you? Same as that night with the Muslims. Awful worried, aren't you?

Michael   For God's sake, he's only a kid.

Mush   He's the biggest kid I ever seen.

Harry   One scrap already and tucks more on the way.

Michael   What happened? . . . Mush?

Mush   The train was in, and they were waiting in The Lion, and we were all having a few –

Harry   Oh, he's no beginner on the beer, Des isn't. I spotted that straightaway. I wonder what he used to do with the money you used send him? Schoolbooks, hah?

Mush   And Des went out to the jacks and we heard the scuffle starting.

Harry   No, he's no beginner on the beer. Are you sure you don't mind him bustin' his pioneer pin? Person'lly, I do.

Mush   And we breezed out lively, Michael, and these two English blokes – one of them putting the nut into Des.

Harry   Terrible job it's going to be, buying pints for Des and brandy for Dada.

Mush   But they seen us coming, and they're scappering lively, and Des is dropping, and one of them, you know, shouting, ''e was lookin' for it,' but Hugo got him a right fong up in the arse as he was running out the passageway. And your father was crabbed as hell when he heard they got away.

Harry   But the place *you* were standing; you could have got the other fella.

Mush   But I swung, Har, on me oath. Didn't you see me? But he was coming this way – see? – and I had to throw the punch with my right. But, normally, I punch with my left, chop with my right, 'cause I can't straighten this little finger – see? – since my accident.

Harry (*quietly amused*)   Hah?

Mush (*laughs*)   Hah-haa, Har! (*Chants.*)
  And Harry struck and Iggy struck
  And Hugo struck and then,
  Upon the floor, all K.O. dead,
  Were the bloody Englishmen!

Michael   Is Des all right?

Harry   The bloody Englishmen, the lousy Englishmen. And there's a lot of lousy Irishmen too. Isn't there?

Mush   Scores of them. They're all the same.

Harry   They're not the same.

Mush   No, oh no, some are different right enough. Some are tougher, like you and Iggy. It's the –

Michael   Is Des all right?

Harry   Don't you hear the man talking? (*To* **Mush**.) They're not the same.

Mush   That's what I was going to say.

Harry   Well, say it.

Mush   It's the fly shams I'm talking about. You have to keep watching them all the time.

Harry   What fly shams?

Mush   Them smiling shams that start doing you favours because they want something off you. And if they don't do something for you, it's because they want something for that too.

Harry   Person'lly, why should a man do nothing for nothing?

Mush   I know, but they deny that, and you don't know where you are. Them fellas in charge say they're running things for what they can put into things. And they're just there for what they –

Harry   Can get out of things.

Mush   That's what has the world daft the way it is.

Harry   I don't mind.

Mush   Neither do I. But that's my opinion. And it's how they put on the serious faces that gets me most of all.

Killed out, making big serious faces, organizing and that. But one little eye is doing a cute slow waltz all the time to see if the big boss, or the priest, or someone sees how killed out they are making faces.

Harry The holy ones is the worst.

Mush The ones that say 'Fawther' – like that: 'Fawther' – to the priest. And their sons is always thick. But they get the good jobstakes all the same. County Council and that.

Harry Them are the ones that gam on not to know you when they meet you.

Mush Even the ones was in your own class.

Michael That's because of the way they think you feel towards them. It's not how they feel. They don't mean –

Harry Thinking so hard when they meet you that they don't see you 'cause they're thinking so deep.

Mush Aw, but we're all equal and love your brother. Pray for them that persecute –

Harry An' calumniate –

Mush And fornicate you. (*They laugh.*)
(*To* **Michael**.) Are you wise to them clients at all?

Michael I –

Harry He knows them.

Michael I know them. But they don't eat me.

Mush Did you ever notice the way they wrinkle up their noses, 'specially when –

Michael There's no need to –

Harry What?

Michael Exaggerate.

Harry He's not. They do. Exaggerating what anyway? You don't know what he was going to say, so how do you know it's exaggerating? See? Your big mistake is thinking they don't do it to you. Go on, Mush. They wrinkle up their noses.

Mush   Yeh know, when they have on their four minx furs, and their crocodile skins shoes, they wrinkle up their noses.

Harry   That's right.

Michael   That's because of the smell of the furs and crocodiles.

Harry (*rejects joke*)   Naw-naw-naw-naw. The British boys! And smiles, looking sideways, and spitting over their left shoulders unknown.

Michael   And Paddies.

Harry   You're not a Paddy?

Michael   We're all Paddies and the British boys know it.

Harry   So we can't disappoint them if that's what they think. Person'lly, I wouldn't disappoint them.

Michael   You won't fit into a place that way.

Harry   Who wants to?

Michael   I do.

Harry   You want to be a British Paddy?

Michael   No. But a lot of it is up to a man himself to fit into a place. Otherwise he might as well stay at home.

Harry   It's up to a man himself?

Mush   It's up to us?

Michael   Give and take.

Mush   Us? We've no chance. Har? Too much back-handin', too much palm-oil, too many Holy Marys pulling strings, and talking about merit.

Harry   Too many people smiling. Too many –

Mush   That's what I was saying.

Harry   Too many people saying hello. Too many –

Mush   That's what I was saying, Har.

Harry   Hah?

Mush   That everyone has a motive these days, even for a smile.

Harry   Hah?

Mush   That's what I was saying a minute ago.

Harry (*considers for a moment*)   Okay. What's your motive for goin 'round with me?

Mush   Hah? . . . Oh, it's . . . Well, we were in the same class. Remember? Me, you and Hugo in the back seat.

Harry   But what are you smiling for? What do you want?

Mush   Aw, jay, sham, don't take it too serious.

Harry   Aw, but I do.

Mush   But it's only with some people, Har, that –

Harry   Yeh. What's Michael's motive?

Mush   For what?

Harry   For anything. For keeping us here.

Mush   God, I don't know. Brothers, ye're all brothers.

Harry   Naw – naw. Why do you do it, Mikey? And, I think, it's you following us. And you don't like us, I think. Hah? Tell us, Mush.

Mush   God, I don't know. I suppose he has no choice.

Harry   Hah? (*Then he laughs.*)

Mush   Aw jay, I didn't mean it like that.

Michael   We have enough bull talk around here.

Mush   Well, I'm just going.

Harry Sit down.

Mush No, honest, the quare one should be waiting this hour. I just want to tell her I'm not available tonight. See you later. The best! Taw! (*Exits.*)

Pause. **Harry** *first, then* **Michael**, *take out cigarettes and each lights one.*

Michael Harry, I wanted to – We should have a talk.

Harry In case you think I'm drunk or something –

Michael No, I wasn't thinking that. I know you're not.

Harry What do you want to talk about?

Michael Well –

Harry Dada, is it?

Michael No, about Des.

Harry What about him?

Michael He's okay?

Harry He's okay.

Michael Well, he's the youngest.

Harry Yeh?

Michael He's only a kid and, well, he couldn't have much sense yet.

Harry He won't be long wising-up over here – What are you getting at?

Michael Well, it's up to the two of us – it's up to us to see he goes home in, say, a week's time.

Harry An' why?

Michael Just, it's up to the two of us. He's only a kid and, well, there's no one left at home now with Mama.

Harry Isn't there Dada?

Michael   Des hasn't a chance over here.

Harry   Chance of what?

Michael   Look at it this way. It'd be sort of all right, wouldn't it, if Des was something? Something in the family.

Harry   Oh yeh, yeh, sure.

Michael   We could be proud of him. Some one of us at last to get something decent, a good job. Everyone has a boast about something. We never had —

Harry   There's Dada, an' —

Michael   Des is still young. He could still get — *something*. We're all — all of us — well, straight talking, we don't count.

Harry   A doctor maybe?

Michael   Something — No — something.

Harry   A solicitor maybe?

Michael   No, just something, respectable, to be at home.

Harry   Crap! Be something like you, is it, afraid of his shadow?

Michael   Wait a minute —

Betty *is standing in kitchen doorway.*

Harry   Then we'd be proud of him, is it? It's up to the two of us, you and me. Crap, daff, bullshit! Do you think I'm an eejit? Des can do what he likes. Anyway he's staying on. We need him.

Michael   I don't mean he has to be a doctor or a — What do you mean you need him?

Harry   Just we need him, that's all. Anyway, he's staying. There's no one forcing him, but he's not going home yet.

Betty   The Mulryans.

Harry   Aaaa, Betty Batter bought a pound of butter! Sly lickle Betty does be earwiggin' at keyholes.

Michael   For God's sake, you're not going to meet the Mulryans?

Betty   Behind the old factory, up Rock's Lane.

Harry   There was an old woman called Betty. You know that one? Mush told me. He knows all them ones.

Michael   Hold on a minute now –

Harry   There was an old woman called Betty, she slipped off the back of the sette; the sette it broke –

Michael   But why?

Harry   Why not?

Michael   Why fight the Mulryans?

Harry   Oh, a lot think, you know, we aren't able for them. But that wouldn't bother you. Just like Dada said, you've no pride.

Michael   Dada is in on this already?

Harry   We told him. The Mulryans was doing a lot of braggin' about what they'd do to us, so we sent them word we was claimin' them. Carneys verses Mulryans. All the Carneys: me, Iggy, Dada, Hugo and Des. Des'll be good. Five of us, seven of them.

Michael   You're crazy. Do you know what you're doing this time? You know the kind they are, how they fight.

Harry   You know how I fight. We're all iron men. Not just Iggy. Ask Dada. Fight all night, Michael. Anyone. (*Holds up his fist.*) Iron, look. Aw, but look, more iron. (*Withdraws from his pocket an ass-shoe which he wears as a knuckle duster. He gives* **Michael** *a tap on the shoulder with it.*) A souvenir from Ireland. Iron, man. Let no one say there was ever a jibber in our family! Or was there? Hah? Not even one? Was there a jibber in our family, Michael? Go on, tell the missus.

Michael   If you have to fight and get killed, don't draw Des into it, that's all.

Harry   Jibber, jibber, what about the jibber?

Michael   That sort of thing doesn't bother me at all.

Harry   Hah?

Betty   And you'd want to start looking for new digs.

Harry   Hah?

Michael   Just don't draw Des into it.

Harry   Hah?

Betty   We're going to do the place up.

Harry   Now, Bitchey, how would you like to keep your English mouth out of it, and let the *man* of the house talk? (*To* **Michael**.) What were you saying? You're tired of us, is it? Mush says you've no choice. What do you think?

Michael   My concern at the moment is for Des.

Betty   You'll just have to get out, that's all.

Harry   Look, why don't you go back to the skivvying in there? (*Men's voices off.*)

Betty   You don't talk to me like that.

Michael   Take it easy.

Harry   You want to talk about Des? Well, I think we should have a talk too, about something else. That night with the Muslims.

Michael   Another time. They're here.

Harry   Two days in hospital.

Michael *opens hall door.* **Iggy**, **Hugo**, **Dada** *and* **Des** *are coming in front door. They come into the living room.* **Dada** *is a* *fine tall man and aware of it. He is about sixty.* **Des** *is a big loose-limbed youth. Very eager to be accepted. At times given to cockiness. At the moment he behaves shyly. His face carries some mark of the fight.*

Harry   We were just talking about ye.

Dada   Hah-ha, yes. How are you, Michael? (*Warm handshake for* **Michael**.)

Michael   You're welcome, ye're welcome. Come in. Don't say this is Des?

Des (*shyly; mutters*)   Michael. (*Clumsy handshake.*)

Dada   That's Desmond.

Michael   I thought you'd be a little lad that size. Come in.

Dada   Thank you.

Michael   Sit down, sit down.

Dada   Thank you.

Michael   Oh, this is my wife, Betty. Betty, this is Dada. And Des.

Dada (*rises, bows, shakes her hand warmly*)   I've heard a lot about you. How do you do, ma'am!

Betty (*impressed by him*)   Mister Carney. (*She shakes hands with* **Des**, *who remains seated.*) How do you do! Let me take your coats.

Michael   Yes, take off your coats.

Dada   I hope we aren't too much trouble, inconvenience.

Betty   Not at all, not at all.

Michael   Not at all.

Betty *takes coats out to hall.*

Dada   Well, you're looking well, Michael. That's a nice woman you got.

Michael   You're looking well yourself.

Dada   Can't help it, can't help it.

Michael   No, I suppose . . . How's Mama? (*Slight pause.* **Dada** *feels there is an accusation in such questions.*)

Dada   . . . Fine, fine. Sent her love. To you all. I wanted her to come over with Desmond and I'd stay at home – Didn't I, Desmond? – Or even come with the two of us, yes, but you know your mother? Somebody might run away with the house. And – Hah-haa!

Michael   . . . Was it rough crossing?

Dada   A bit, a bit. (*Chuckles.*) Desmond didn't feel too good. It didn't affect an old sailor like me though.

Michael   No.

Betty   Will I get the tea now?

Michael   Oh yes, do, do.

Dada (*rising*)   Don't go to any trouble now, ma'am. Just a cup.

Betty (*exiting to kitchen*)   It's no trouble at all, Mr Carney.

Dada   Yes, nice woman you got, Michael.

Michael   I'd hardly know Des, honestly: he's got so big. How are things with you, Des?

Des   Good.

Dada   He has shoulders like the old man all right, hasn't he?

Michael   It must be hard trying to keep a lad like that fed at home.

Dada (*slight pause*)   . . . We want for nothing at home.

Michael (*quickly*)   I know, I know. Just coddin' about Des growing so much. (**Dada** *looks at* **Harry**, **Iggy** *and*

Hugo.) Oh, a thing I was often thinking about. Then trees we planted. Do you remember? Did they grow?

Des   Oh, yeh.

Michael   Before I – before I came over here, Des and myself were down in the wood one day and we got these five young ash trees. And we planted them at the wall at the back of the house. Five of them, one for each of us, five sons, you know. I was wondering, did they all grow?

Des   They did. I think. Some of them.

Dada   I never seen them. It's dangerous anyway having trees near a house like that.

Hugo   Storms and all.

Dada   Not only that, but the carbon dioxide. Gas. The trees give it out at night. The carbon dioxide. Tid poison you. (*The sons, except* **Michael**, *provide a good audience for this sort of thing from* **Dada**.)

Michael   What are you at now?

Dada   Ah – Work, is it?

Michael   Yeh.

Dada   Something lined up, you know.

Michael   Yeh?

Dada   Yes. A good job on the way. (*Slight pause.*) Hah-haa! You never lost it, Michael. The old worrier. Isn't he the old worrier, lads? (*Inviting them to laugh with him.*) Isn't he the old worrier?

Michael (*to* **Des**)   What do you think of Coventry?

Hugo   Dother way round: what does Coventry think of him, eh, Dessie? (**Des** *feels the bruise on his face.*)

Dada   Yes, Coventry has made its impression already.

Michael   Is it okay?

Des   Nothing. Two fellas in the – the, yeh know, of the pub. And they were laughing, yeh know, and talking about – well, Paddies.

Hugo   Wait'll you hear this. Go on, Des.

Des   Sort of jybin', well, sort of jybin' Iggy and Hugo. They must have been listening to us inside. And I sort of went across to them and I said, 'Well, I'm a Paddy', I said –

Michael   You shouldn't have taken any notice of –

Harry ⎫   Go on, Des.
Hugo ⎭   Shush!

Des   Well, they went for me. Well, I had to defend myself. Well, I had to try to. Two of them. One of them sort of came at me with his head, his forehead –

Hugo   The nut –

Des   And I got this. (*Bruise.*) And stars for a minute, and then, well, lights out. (*All except* **Michael** *laugh.*)

Dada   I wish I was there when it happened. Paddies! Irish people talk better than English people do.

Hugo   And O'Connell Street is the widest street in – in the world.

Dada   But wait a minute, Desmond. You said, well I'm a Paddy, right?

Des   I said –

Dada   And where were you standing then?

Des   Well, I was – Well, I went across, and they were – you know? –

Dada   But you were standing in the middle of the – the – the toilet?

Des   They were sort of – You know? And –

Dada   And they went for you, right?

Des   Well, they were – ah – and I let go just when –

Dada   But you didn't connect proper?

Des   I –

Dada   Properly –

Des   They were coming for me, and I –

Dada   They tore into you. What did you do then?

Des   When they – ?

Dada   Yes, rushed you.

Des   I – they – well, his head –

Dada   You waited for them, right?

Des   I –

Dada   Wrong. Wrong, lad. Big mistake. You should have – Well, ask Ignatius, Henry. I bet they'd agree. You shouldn't have stood there.

Hugo   Called us.

Dada   No. I'm surprised at you, Hubert. Your back to the wall, man. Protection, the wall, your back to it. Ignatius?

Iggy   No one behind you.

Dada   Your back to the wall.

Iggy   And keep swingin'.

Dada   Remember that now. You won't always have me or your brothers. So what do you do?

Des   Get back to the wall – and keep swingin'.

Dada   And a last piece of advice. Don't ever go expecting anyone, a friend or anyone, to help you in a fight. While you're looking around for that friend, you could be finished. If someone joins in, okay, but you keep your eyes on your man.

Harry   And if someone joins in, you don't run.

Des   But I wouldn't.

Dada   There's good stuff in Desmond.

Des   I wouldn't.

Dada   No fear of him doing that.

Harry (*looks at* **Michael**)   Just in case he might be another four-minute sham.

Des   I know a thing or two.

Harry   I know. (*Looks at* **Michael**.) We've a sort of joke here about sprinters.

Michael (*exiting to kitchen*)   Is the tea ready? (**Dada** *winks at* **Michael**'s *back for the quiet amusement of the others.*)

Harry   Did you not see the bottle? (**Des** *looks at him.*) . . . On the little windowsill. Dust and cobwebs on it. Did you not see it? What was that doing there?

Iggy   Hard hittin's enough.

Harry   Naw-naw, a bottle is better than a fist. A broken bottle is better than two fists. See the fear of God it puts into them and they start backin' away from you.

Iggy   I seen fellas fightin' better because of the fear of God.

Harry   Naw, not with the spikey glass in front of their eyes. They don't know what to do they're so frightened. And he tries to save himself with his hands, and they get bleeding first –

Michael (*entering with some tea things*)   Take it easy, Harry –

Harry   You pay attention, Des –

Michael   Take it easy –

Harry   Michael, our miler, don't like glass, he don't like blood, he don't like us, he don't like anything!

Iggy   W-w-what if you've no bottle, what then?

Harry   Always this. (*Produces the ass-shoe.*)

Hugo   Or a chain or a rasp or a belt or a chair.

Harry   You pay attention, Des. You be my 'prentice and I'll make you a tradesman, a good 'un.

Michael   Come on, the tea is getting cold.

Harry   Which is best you think, Dada, bottles or just fists? Is Iggy or me right?

Michael   Dada, stow it. This kind of talk is –

Dada   Aw, this is a good healthy argument. It could save a man's life. Now, fists or bottles. Well, when I was your age I could flatten any man that came my way with my fists. Hah-haa, Ignatius! And I still can, make no mistake about that. One man, two men or three men. After that – Hah-haa, Harry! – I see no harm in taking up a – a club to even up the numbers. Do you get me now?

Harry   Why take the risk ever, fighting fair with anyone?

Dada   It's up to yourself. Can you take him without a club?

Harry   Why ask the question at all?

Dada   Yes.

Harry   Hah? A fight's a fight, Dada.

Hugo   That's right.

Harry   Hah?

Dada   That's right. It's a very personal question, and up to the man involved.

Betty (*entering with tea things*)   Would you like to sit at the table now?

Dada   Thank you, ma'am.

Harry   Hah?

Dada   Ah, the tea! (**Dada** *and* **Des** *start to eat.*)

Betty   Tea, Harry? (**Harry** *ignores her.*)

Dada   Very tasty. You're a very good cook, ma'am.

Betty   Oh, I would like to have done something nicer for you, Mr Carney.

Dada   Very tasty. (**Betty** *exits to the kitchen.*) Yes, very nice woman you got there, Michael.

Mush (*enters*)   God bless the work! Is Harry here? (*Sees* **Harry**.) One of your long-haired ones is waiting up the road.

Dada   Are you courting, Henry?

The others laugh. **Harry** *scowls.*

Mush (*to* **Dada**)   I hear things are very bad in Mary Horan's country, Mr Carney?

Dada   What?

Michael   Ireland: Mary Horan's country.

Mush   The economy destroyed since the demand for St Patrick's day badges fell. (*They laugh. To* **Harry**.) Bhuil tú ag teacht? (**Harry** *exits, followed by* **Mush**. *As he goes out:*) Slán libh!

Dada   Slán leat!

Betty (*entering from kitchen with a bowl of fruit*)   I've just put on some more food, Mr Carney, it won't take long.

Hugo   Can you talk Irish, Dada?

Dada   I'm fluent at it. Many's the conversation I have at home with John Quinlan. You know, John, the doctor. And Anthony Heneghan – he's an architect. At the club.

And often, for the sport of it, we talk nothing but Irish all night. At the club.

Michael   I think I knew Anthony Heneghan.

Dada   A grand young man, scholarly, fond of his jar.

Michael   He was a few years ahead of me at school.

Dada   You should have gone on for an architect.

Michael   Two years in a secondary school wouldn't have made an architect out of me.

Dada   Your aunt would have kept you on at that school, but instead you kept running back to us every chance you got. I didn't think you were that fond of us in them days. Hah, lads? (*Smiles at the others.*) But it's a grand job though, an architect, and plenty of cash in it. And nothing to it. Even Anthony admits that. Sure, anyone can draw a house.

Michael (*to* **Des**)   How long do ye think ye'll stay?

Dada   I'll take a week, maybe ten days, to see ye're all okay.

Michael (*to* **Des**)   Yeh?

Des   I think I'll stay another while. I'll get something here to keep me going. Harry said he'd fix me up anyway.

Michael   I thought you were getting into the new factory at home?

Des   A lousy few quid. I don't fancy it much.

Dada   The lad has the wandering bug too. Do you think you'd like it here, Desmond?

Michael   It'd be better for you at home.

Dada   I thought you two used to get on well.

Des   I think I'll try it for a while, Michael.

Dada   Now you want to send him back, and he's just over.

Michael   Wouldn't it be all right for you to have someone at home?

Dada   I didn't think I looked that old. Do I, boys?

Michael   Well, for Mama then.

Dada   Naturally we want to keep the boy, but I wouldn't keep a lad from what he wants himself, just for walking around the house. Amn't I right? That was always my way. Free will.

Des   There's too many bosses in that factory job. Slave-drivers. You don't have to lick no one's shoes over here.

Michael   No one would like it better than me for you to be over here, but the job at home is sound, secure.

Dada   Why are you putting him off?

Michael   There isn't a lot over here for anyone, Dada. At home is a better bet.

Dada   You're casting a reflection on your brothers, Michael.

Michael   He could go to the Tech and all at night, Dada. Don't you agree? And then, maybe later –

Dada   The trouble with you, Michael, is you've no pride. I don't want people, twopence-halfpenny guys, ordering a son of mine, a Carney, to clean up after them.

Michael   I'm not going again' you now, Dada, but what do you think he'll be doing over here?

Dada   I'm not a man that believes in apron-strings. Desmond is the youngest, but he's no child. I let the rest of you make your own choices, decisions. Free will. Always believed in that. So, if you failed, you can't blame me. They were your own decisions. Oh, but you didn't fail, and I'm proud, and you did it on your own. No matter who is casting suspicious reflections. I was always a proud man, everyone will tell you that. I have my pride, I know, but, as I said, a man must have prude. And, in the words of the great Gene Tunney, a man must fight back. His father was a Mayoman too.

Michael (*to* **Iggy**)   What do you think, should he stay or go?

Iggy   Not my affair.

Michael   A straight answer.

Hugo   We need him.

Michael (*to* **Iggy**)   Does he know what for?

Iggy   Let her (**Des**) do the choosing. Like Dada said, she's no baby.

Des   I'd like to stay, Michael; honest.

Michael   Don't be a fool. You don't know what's here for you.

Hugo   He isn't a fool.

Des   I'm needed. This is for the family.

Dada   Well said.

Des   It wouldn't be fair if I went back. The Mulryans. Seven of them. I don't think it'd be fair to back out. Anyway, I wouldn't.

Dada   No, it wouldn't be right. If the Mulryans is bragging about what they'd do to sons of mine, then they have to be learned different. Differently.

Michael   And when is this great event to take place?

Iggy   Any time they like.

Hugo   We sent them word.

Dada   And I'm proud of ye, your ability, as my father was proud of me; afraid of no man, able for all.

Michael   A fine man isn't a thug.

Dada   Any man can't fight isn't worth his salt. I'm restraining myself, Michael. A man must fight back at – at – at – A man must fight back. I'm a fighting man myself, and I can talk with the best, and mix with them. And as Anthony Heneghan said to me one evening –

Michael   This is no place for another Carney.

Dada   What? . . . Aren't we not welcome here? I told ye, didn't I, he'd start it.

Michael   I'm not starting anything. Dada, listen –

Dada   Don't tell me to listen! It wasn't easy for me to come here, but I came. That's me, forgive and forgot, all for the sake of the family. I came here in good faith, and the welcome I get is a barrage of insinuating questions.

Michael   All I'm asking is a simple thing.

Dada   No!

Michael   No one said anything about good faith.

Dada   Are you sneering at what I'm saying? At your father. Do ye see him, lads?

Michael   Honest to God! All I'm saying is –

Dada   Do ye hear him?

Michael   Should Des go home. I think it's better.

Dada   And whom is the rightful judge on that matter?

Michael   God, that's exactly what you used to say to me fifteen years ago.

Dada   I'm not welcome boys.

Hugo   By God, he won't throw no one out and me here.

Michael   Who said anything about that? I just said –

Des   I can take care of myself, honest, Michael.

Dada   No, he knows better, Desmond.

Michael   What am I?

Dada   What? What are you saying?

Michael   What's Harry? (*Points to* **Iggy** *and* **Hugo**.) What are they? And what's he going to be? (**Des.**) What are we, the Carneys?

Dada   Oh, I've my pride if you haven't. As I said –

Michael } And what are –
Dada   } I'm afraid of no man alive and I can talk with the best and –

Michael   What are you?

Dada   . . . There's no change in you. We're rotten – the lot of us – except you.

Michael   It's not my fault.

Dada   And is it mine?

Hugo   Dada's first night over. No one should talk to their father like that.

Dada   No, Hubert, they shouldn't. But he's our educated boy. I thought we were rid of you years ago when I flung you out, but you keep sticking on.

Hugo   He that asked us to stay here.

Dada   He wants to live with men, and he hasn't a gut in his body. Worse, he wants to give the orders. You! You're like a mangy dog: the more it's kicked, the harder it sticks on. That's you! And he calls ye rotten. Him! It's a good job I came over. And you're saying Desmond is going home?

Michael   No need to get excited.

Dada   Wha'? What!

Michael   There's no one trying to give orders. I just want us all to get on. We're a family, and –

Dada   And who is disrupting the family?

Michael   No need to get excited.

Dada   Don't try a bluff! You should know it won't work with me. You can talk a bit, but you can't act. Actions speak louder than words. The man of words fails the man of action. Or maybe you have changed, got brave? Maybe you'll act?

Des   I think you're both getting worked up about nothing.

Dada   You don't know him.

Michael   Who do you think you are?

Dada   The same man I always was.

Michael   This isn't twenty years ago.

Dada (*takes off his belt*)   The same belt even. Look.

Michael   Are you mad? This is my house you're in now, remember.

Dada   Aw, aren't you great to have a house, doing well. We're proud of you. Is it paid for though? It doesn't change things whose house it is. Or maybe you are the boss here, what? Instead of your faithful dog look. Any more instructions, doggie, any more sneering?

Betty *is entering with tray of food.*

Michael   We're all grown up. We're not kids now.

Dada   *We're? We're?* I'm talking to you! You, on your own! Are you grown up over us?

Michael   You can't walk in here and –

Dada *sees* **Betty***: he hesitates for a moment – embarrassed – then he lashes the table with his belt savagely; he feels he has let himself down; it drives him to excesses.*

Dada   Up, muck and trash, we'll put him to bed like in the old days!

Iggy *and* **Hugo** *stand, one each side of* **Dada**. *The whole attitude is threatening.* **Michael** *shakes his hands, meaning calm down, and exits hall door.* **Betty** *follows.* **Dada** *hesitates, then laughs harshly after* **Betty**.

Dada   Hah-haaaa! . . . I showed him. He never changed a bit. Like old times! (*He throws his arms around* **Hugo** *and* **Iggy**.) But do ye know I was very lonely for ye at home. I'm glad I came. I'm glad. Yes. Aa, ye're great lads. (**Des**, *seated, is looking up at them.*)

Act Two

The following night.

Dada *is viewing himself from different angles in the mirror. But eventually he is standing motionless, his face hopeless, looking at himself in the mirror.* **Michael** *is heard coming down the stairs.* **Dada** *reacts indecisively. Eventually, a moment of childish defiance when he takes out a cigar and considers lighting it. He changes his mind and puts it back in his pocket.* **Michael** *enters. He wants to speak to* **Dada***. He adjusts his tie unnecessarily, recombs his hair, finds a handkerchief in the sideboard. The silence goes on, though it is obvious that both of them would like to talk. Eventually,* **Dada** *exits, whistling tunelessly.* **Michael** *is annoyed that the opportunity for a private talk has passed. Then* **Dada** *re-enters, and starts with a blurt.*

Dada   For the sake of the family – ah – Wish to – to – to. Friction a bad thing domestically, a bad thing. . . . Yes. (**Michael** *is delighted. He doesn't know how to begin. He opens his mouth to speak.*) No. Sufficient said. Yes. Internal friction always bad domestically. Yes.

Michael   . . . Will you smoke, Dada?

Dada   No, I'll smoke – (*His hand to his pocket for cigar. He changes his mind.*) Ah – I will. Thank you. (**Michael** *lights cigarettes.*) Thank you. (*Pause.*) Very nice cigarette. (*Pause.*)

Dada } I hope –
Michael } I wanted to –

Dada   Yes?

Michael   No, Dada, what were you going to say?

Dada   Oh, just, I – I hope you appreciate the moral courage it took for me to – Duty.

Michael   Yes, I do.

Dada   It wasn't easy for me to – Internal friction bad – and –

Michael   Yes, I know, I appreciate it.

Dada   Duty.

Michael   Yes.

Dada   Family.

Michael   Yes. That's what I wanted to talk about too.

Dada (*wary*)   Well, maybe we should postpone – What?

Michael   It's a good few years – It's a long time since we saw you, and – Well, we weren't home for a long time.

Dada   Yes?

Michael   We're changed more than you know.

Dada   Do you think so, son?

Michael   You haven't – I mean, the others. They've gone completely –

Dada   Spirited.

Michael   No. They're big names.

Dada   Big names?

Michael   No, I don't mean in that sense.

Dada   Carneys.

Michael   I mean, around this area. And I was getting a bit worried, and I moved out here too. You know?

Dada   Henry is talking about buying a car.

Michael   I thought I could sober them up.

Dada   A lot of prestige attached to a car.

Michael   Straight talking, Dada. Harry has a couple of women working for him. You know, you know what I mean. He even suggested I give him the front room for his – business. And Iggy is foreman of a heavy-digging job just outside town, and under Harry's supervision he sacks and hires Harry's clients, mostly darkies and men that find it hard to get work. And then, every pay-day, they collect a pound or two apiece off all that Iggy hired.

Dada   They're in it in a big way?

Michael   No. It's not that big. They're trying to be fly, they think they're being fly. There's no one to tell them.

Dada   They could be big.

Michael   No. It's where it's all leading to.

Dada   You wouldn't turn down a soft pound.

Michael   I know, I know. I'm as light-fingered as anyone. But it's a can of paint, a bit of timber, a few bricks –

Dada   Make your money fast. It's the only way. That's the way they all did it. Then buy a business. The whole family could be in on it. Michael Carney & Sons. Hah-haa, Michael Carney *Senior* & Sons.

Michael   Sure, I know, it'd be great, but –

Dada   What?

Michael   Well, the police –

Dada (*snaps*)   What about them? I know about the police. I was one myself.

Michael   But it's where it's all leading to. And I've this awful feeling that something terrible is going to happen.

Dada   No danger. I'm very fast to size up a good thing, opportunity. Cute Henry never said a word about his enterprises.

Michael   Do you know what it is –

Dada   Michael G. Carney & Sons, over a shop, Michael.
There's plenty of time for respectability when we've
showed them.

Michael   Do you know what I mean when I say he has a
few little girls working for him? Kids. I see them down the
road in the little café. Don't you know what it is to take a
couple of quid off a workingman every week?

Dada   Make – the – most – of – opportunity.

Michael   No. No! And you know this is terrible the same
as I do.

Dada   They're the only ones at it, are they?

Michael   No, but –

Dada   Well, then –

Michael   No.

Dada (*viciously*)   And – what – do – you – think – I –
should – do?

Michael   Well, the first thing –

Dada   Drag Desmond home behind me?

Michael (*pauses, considering this*)   . . . It's just I have this
awful feeling. Well, maybe I shouldn't have brought that
up last night. Just as you said, he's no child now. And he's
bright enough. And let him have a look around for a while,
and then decide for himself.

Dada   So I'm not the fool you think I am?

Michael   I never thought that. The first thing is that
fight with the Mulryans.

Dada   Don't fight?

Michael   You know yourself what can happen.

Dada   I don't know.

Michael   You wouldn't be doing it for me, Dada.

Dada   Oh-ho-no, I wouldn't be doing it for you. I never did anything for you, did I?

Michael   No, I don't mean that. You're the only one they'll listen to.

Dada   I know.

Michael   Well, look, do you honestly – A straight question now – Do you honestly think they should fight?

Dada   Enough said. You're always right, I'm always wrong, the defaulter. No, say no more. My advice and views –

Michael   Stay a minute –

Dada   Are respected, sought by the best everywhere, anywhere I go. But you know it all.

Michael   Well, what are you going to do about it?

Dada   I've no more time for you. I know how you think. I came in here like a man to – to – to – And this is the reception. (*Takes out his cigar and holds it up defiantly.*)

Michael   Well, what are you going to do?

Dada   Enough said. My responsibility, boy, my responsibility. (*Exits upstairs.*)

Betty *and* **Des** *enter.*

Betty (*throwing herself into a chair*)   Phew! It's warm outside. Des and I were going to go off somewhere for the night, Michael. Weren't we?

Des (*laughs*)   Yeh.

Betty   What do you think of that, Michael?

Michael (*absently*)   Yeh.

Betty (*to* **Des**)   Wouldn't you like to be as handsome as your brother?

Des (*laughs*)   Yeh.

Michael (*irritably*)   Then you could get a pretty little woman like me: English.

Betty   We must get a nice girl for you, Des. I know! That pretty girl in the paper shop on the corner. Yes, I think she would be –

Michael (*angrily*)   Why are you always trying to organize other people? Do you think they don't know how to organize their own lives? What business is it of yours? (*Realizes he is being unfair; he tries to pass it off.*) Des is in no hurry with the birds, are you? Don't be in any hurry to go to the altar. See what happened to me.

Des   About fifteen years' time.

Betty   Oh no, you'll be too old then, you'll be past it, like your brother. (**Des** *laughs*.) But when you do get married, make sure –

Michael   You don't see your mother-in-law too often. Mum and Dad. Make sure –

Betty   There's worse than mother-in-laws you can see too often.

Michael   What?

Betty   I said there's worse than mother-in-laws to have around.

Des   Wives.

Michael (*laughs*)   Good boy, Dessie.

Betty   That's very funny, I'm sure.

Michael   Oh-ho, she's getting narked.

Betty   No, I'm not. It would take more than that – not like some. My advice to you is don't get married at all. Honestly, Irishmen shouldn't. (*Exits and goes upstairs.*)

Michael   By gum, lad, hah?

Des   Is she crabbed? (*Upset.*)

Michael   No. (*Sighs; then:*) . . . I just seem to be thinking a bit different from other people these days.

Des   Dada? We saw him going up the stairs when we came in.

Michael   Talk about a man!

Des   Ary, he's all right. He's contrary at times, and, often, he isn't so practical. But it's always the way with clever men. (**Michael** *looks at him but lets him talk on.*) You know how it is. And he finds it hard to talk about little things. And a strange thing, about a month ago, he stole an overcoat. . . . Yes! Dada.

Michael   He never did anything like that before.

Des   I know. And he stole it out of that golf club, where he likes to drink. And it was that Anthony Heneghan's coat. And he just threw it over a wall coming home. I don't know why. He didn't want the coat.

Michael   And did anything happen?

Des   No. But he can't drink there any more. He doesn't know we heard about it, Mama and I. (*Pause.*)

Michael   How is she?

Des   Oh, she's – she's fine.

Michael   How are you fixed for dust?

Des   I'm okay.

Michael   Here's a few quid anyway. You might want something.

Des   No, I'm okay, honest.

Michael (*pushes money into* **Des**'s *top pocket*)   Here, take it, don't be silly. If you're stuck later let me know. You might want to get something for Mama.

Des   Thanks.

Michael   She's all right, is she?

Des   Yeh. Fine. She said to tell you come home for Christmas.

Michael   I might.

Des   No, she said to be sure you come. To tell you.

Michael   I might all right.

Des   She said even for a few days.

Michael   It's over ten years, yeh know.

Des   God, it'd be great. Wouldn't it be great if we were all at home together at Christmas? Walking up town, us all together. I think she gets sort of lonely. Us all gone, you know.

Michael   Yeh.

Des   I think she gets sort of lonely.

Michael (*getting irritable*)   Yes. He never made things easy for her. He – (*Restrains himself.*)

Des   Well, he got a fair amount of tough luck, like. But you'd manage a few days anyway, and try and pull with himself. He can be understanding too.

Michael (*reflectively*)   Yeh. I never thought he was stupid. If he was I wouldn't mind. Just getting dafter. Not stupid. Just hare-brained.

Harry *and* **Mush** *enter.*

Harry   Who's hair-brains? You it must be, Mush, they're talking about.

Mush   Not me, I'm a rabbit man myself. Remember the rabbit, Har? God made the bees and –

Harry   The bees made honey;

Mush   God made man and –

Harry   Man made money –

Mush   God made the rabbit to run around the grass –

Harry ⎱ God made the greyhound to catch him by the
Mush ⎰ arse.

Harry   I hear that Dada is a bit of a greyhound too,
though, hah? I hear he can still make you run.

Michael   How're the Flanagans, Des?

Des   The ones used to live next door?

Michael   Used?

Des   They moved into a new house a few years ago.
(**Michael** *nods to* **Harry**.)

Harry (*copies the nod*)   What's that supposed to mean?

Michael   They've a new house.

Harry   Yeh?

Mush (*laughs*)   Pookey Flanagan. That's what we used
call him. He used sweep the roads.

Michael   That's right. He was a road-sweeper. And one
of his sons became an engineer, and there was a girl that
became a nun, and another of them was at the university
when I left. All from the dirt of the roads.

Harry   Yeh, that's very interesting.

Michael   But you were saying yesterday, as far as I
remember, that people like us haven't a chance to get on.

Harry   I didn't say that *I'm* not getting by, did I, in my
own special little person'l way, did I?

Michael   And what was Dada?

Des   A policeman once.

Michael   Yeh.

Harry   Yeh what?

Michael   And what's that old saying of yours, Mush:
'Why wouldn't he get on, a policeman's son?' We're a
policeman's sons.

Harry Dada did all right as far as I'm concerned.

Michael Roaring around the town, louder than someone shouting the water is to be turned off, that the Carneys are the best men?

Mush Times were hard, Michael, in them days.

Michael Harder for Pookey Flanagan.

Harry Why you trying to knock him? You think he belted you too much? Person'lly I don't think you ever got belted enough.

Michael I'd just like some people to know that a lot of the rubbish talked isn't the gospel.

Harry (*looks at* **Des**) Hah?

Des I hear about the old days even yet.

Michael They're hard to live down.

Des No, a lot of people at home talk about Iggy – and ye all – with a sort of respect. They do, Michael. And they know Iggy is called the Iron Man over here. Even outside the town, they're, well – kind of afraid of the name Carney.

Michael Afraid?

Harry Afraid.

Mush I'd agree with that.

Des They sort of look up to it.

Michael Come off it. Who looks up to us? I'll tell you – I could tell you a million things.

Harry Yeh, you're clever.

Michael I was up town one day with another fella, and we were passing Doonan's. You know, Doonan, the postman. And his kids were playing outside. And one of them hit the other with a stone, just as we were passing. And Doonan came out. He didn't ask who did it or anything, but when he saw me he shouted, 'Go home, you tinker! Go back to your tent, Carney!' He never asked the kids, he never looked at the fella with me. I was the tinker.

Harry Yeh? An' what did you do?

Michael Well, I didn't think there was any point in saying anything to a man like –

Harry What would you do, Des?

Des I'd have split him wide open, I would! Give him cause to call names.

Michael And then you have another incident chalked up for –

Des But you didn't start it.

Harry That wouldn't worry *him*.

Michael But you were saying there was respect.

Harry You're a coward, that's all.

Michael But you were saying they look up to us. (*Looks at* **Mush**.) *Hah? Hah*, Mush? Do *you*, *hah*, look up to us, *hah*?

Mush Hah? (*Short pause*.) . . . Hah-haa, Har! Remember McQuaide, the school-teacher? (*He starts to cavort about imitating the mannerisms of the school-teacher, and mimicking him*.) Come here to me, O'Reilly! Come out heere, you moron! Aa, look at heem! Look at the cut of heem, boys! Thy knees have seen water at Baptism last! Aa, he thinks it's funny heemself! (*Grabs his cheek between thumb and forefinger, slapping the other cheek with his free hand*.) Now – now – now! The eembecile finds heemself funny! Where's your learned friend? Mr Henry Carney, we'll have your catechism. Up – up – up, wheen I speak to you! Who made the world?

Des MacAlpine! (*They laugh. Then* **Harry** *takes a knife off the table and lifts locks of* **Mush**'s *hair with it*.)

Harry He ever do that to you?

Mush (*a little frightened*)   Yeh.

Harry   To see if they was any lice, fleas, on you, hah?

Mush   Yeh.

Harry (*to* **Michael**)   But, I suppose, he never done it to you?

Michael   Teachers have to –

Harry   Why do they only have to do it to some? You'd imagine – They're teachers! – Polite! – Polite to do it to everyone. Any time I got pox or crabs, wasn't off the ones I thought I'd get it off. Lifting your hair like that. Holding his breath in your ear. Then munchin' them nuts, moving on to the next place in your head, and slobbery bits of white nuts slobbering outside his lips.

Mush   And the oranges, Har.

Harry   He was a pig!

Mush   And the little pen-knife he had for peeling his apples.

Harry   And asking you what you had for your dinner – Not because he cared. And person'l questions. (*Releases* **Mush**. *To* **Michael**.) He never asked you, I suppose?

Michael   Yes.

Harry   Yeh – yeh – yes. He asked all the class one day. 'What you going to be when you grow up?' Some said –

Mush   Yeh! I said that day a lighthouse keeper. And he said –

Harry   Some said engine drivers, and things. And Dada was then sort of selling things round the countryside. Suits and coats and ties and things. Well, just when he came to my turn, and I was ready to say what I was going to be, he said first, 'I suppose, Carney, you'll be a Jewman.' (*Pedlar.*)

Des   What were you going to say anyway you'd be?

Harry (*sincerely*)   Priest. (*Then he looks defiantly at them.*)
. . . I said it too, after he saying the other thing, and he
laughed.

Mush   The friggin' bastard.

Harry   Yeh. The friggin' pig. And all the other friggin'
pigs. (*Suddenly, to* **Michael**.) You'd still salute McQuaide?

Michael   I haven't lost any sleep over him for years.
Would *you* still salute him?

Harry (**Michael** *has found a mark*)   Aw, Jesus, you're very
clever! No – no – naaw, I wouldn't! I fight!

Michael   And what good is that? Be called an Iron Man?

Harry   No!

Michael   Why so?

Harry   Ary why – why – why? – Why my arse – Why
anything?

Michael   But you've no reason, see.

Harry   But, see, I have! I have reasons, see, all right! I'll
fight anyone that wants to, that don't want to! I'm not
afraid of nobody! They don't just ignore me! They don't
ask me what I had for my dinner! They don't –

Des   They? Who?

Harry   Oh, they – they – they – they – THEM! Them
shams! You all know who I'm talking about. You know
them. You know them. He knows them. (*To* **Michael**.)
You suck up to them, I fight them. Who do they think
most of, me or you?

Michael   If it comes to that –

Harry   Aw, do they now? They think more of you? I can
make them afraid. What can you do? They notice me, do
they notice you? They don't pretend to notice me, *but they
do*. And they're beginning to notice me more and more.
And they know clean and straight where I stand. And I

know where I stand. And I like it. And I'm pleased. Person'lly, I'm very pleased. (*Exits to kitchen.*)

Michael   I'm going up to a club up the road. Do you want to come? I won't be long.

Des   I've to give Dada a shout. We're all going out.

Michael *exits. As he goes out,* **Iggy** *and* **Hugo** *are coming in the front door.*

Hugo (*in the hall*)   Well, Killer! (**Iggy** *and* **Hugo** *come into the room.*) Heigh-up! Where's the preacher off to all spruced up?

Mush   Up to Father Rowan's place. I'd better be off myself.

Hugo (*laughs. To* **Iggy**)   That's the place they put you out of one night, and you broke the billiard table first.

Iggy (*in agreement, 'Aw'*)   Aw. Snakes 'n' ladders place.

Harry (*off, in kitchen*)   Where you off to, Mush?

Mush   Ye're all dolled-up beside me, Har. Down to get a clean under-pants: you'd never know who'd you'd meet on a Sunday night.

Harry   See you in The Bower later.

Mush   Right. Taw! The best! (*Exits.*)

Harry (*enters eating a sandwich. To* **Des**)   You didn't go off with Michael? (*And doesn't wait for a reply; to* **Iggy**.) Ye go to the pictures?

Iggy   Aw.

Hugo   Them singing shams is all played out. All mouths and firing roses at women. (*Has been trying to make the television work.*) You'd think he'd get this fixed again. This is a very bad stable we're in. (*Sees* **Harry** *eating. Goes out to the kitchen.*)

Iggy   D'ye remember that kiddie, Hopalong Cassidy? You never see her now.

Hugo (*off, in kitchen*)   He was a tough-un.

Iggy   (I) Used like her.

Hugo (*off*)   I never seen him in a bad picture. Did ye ever notice he used never bother with the women? I never seen him kiss a jane once.

Harry   I did. Just once though. Yeh see, in this picture, this one was after getting shot, and she was dying, out on the prairie, and Hoppy come along, singing or laughing at something, or admiring the view for himself. On his horse. And she was dying. So he seen her, and he jumped down. And she said, 'Hoppy, kiss me, I'm dying', or something.

Hugo (*entering, eating a sandwich*)   Hah?

Harry   'Hoppy, kiss me, I'm dying' – Something.

Hugo   And did he?

Harry   He did.

Hugo   Well, I suppose he couldn't help it.

Iggy   I seen that one! And Hoppy – Well, she nearly started crying, and grinding her teeth, like that. Aw yes, she was the kiddie. Used like her.

Hugo   Where's Dada?

Des   I'd better give him a shout. I don't think he's so flush with the money.

Hugo   We sent him nothing for a few weks.

They start a 'whip round' – **Harry**, **Iggy** *and* **Hugo** *contributing a few pounds each.* **Des** *is going to call* **Dada**. *He opens the door, and* **Dada** *is found standing outside, in the hall.*

Des   Oh, I was just –

Dada (*ignores* **Des**. *Enters*)   Boys, nothing like forty winks in the evening. (*Sees money on the table*.) Oh? Has someone too much money?

Harry   That's yours.

Iggy   You must have left it there.

Hugo   We all chipped in.

Harry *exits to the kitchen*.

Dada   Boys, it's hard not to say a few words at times like this. I know it's not necessary – I am sure of that – nevertheless, permit me. And, unaccustomed as I am to public speaking, I know you realize it is your duty, and you do it in this way of contribution.

Hugo   We can afford it – me, Iggy and Harry.

Des   Well, I –

Dada   All right, Desmond. It isn't expected of you yet.

Hugo   Does Michael ever come across?

Dada   Hubert, it's not 'coming across' when you send me or give me money – When you send it to your mother and I. You all learned your Catechism. Well, honour thy father and thy mother. And when you send me, thy father, money, your honour. Do you get me?

Hugo   We'll squeeze Michael a bit. He'll chip in any more.

Dada   I want nothing of him. And, anyway if I wanted him squeezed, who would I get to do it? Who? Me! – Myself! – The old man! . . . (*They laugh*.) He's gone out, is he? Were you talking to him?

Des   For a while.

Dada   About me?

Des   No.

Dada   What was he saying?

Des   Nothing.

Dada   That's a highly intelligent way of talking. I bet he told you I was – Well, imagine. What else did he say?

Des   He just said ye didn't get on so well.

Dada   And that it's my fault? Get wise to him, he said, to me and your brothers. Well, I'm telling you now, you get wise to him, boy. He tried the same game with Ignatius and Hubert, didn't he? Yes. But they were too smart for him. Looking-down-his-nose act, sneering. Nobody can be right, only him. But I'll do for him yet. He knows a lot, I'm sure.

Des   But, I think, you've got him – well, a bit wrong. He's – Well, he's not too bad.

Dada   Amn't I saying he's an ungrateful tramp. Disrupting. After all I did for him. Amn't I telling you –

Mush (*enters*)   Where's Harry? Where's Harry? They're up at The Lion! They're here! – Where's Harry?

Harry (*comes out of the kitchen, drinking a glass of milk. He remains deliberately casual*)   Hah?

Mush   The Mulryans. They're up at The Lion.

Harry   Yeh?

Mush   I was pointed out. And the first thing I know, the big fella, John, come over behind me and was saying, 'I'll have a pint, mate.'

Harry   Yeh?

Mush   I did. And he said, 'You a friend of the Carneys?' Yeh. 'You know where they live?' Yeh – Yeh, 'Well, run down and tell them, any time.'

Hugo   R-r-r-right.

Harry   No rush. They're drinking?

Mush   He swallowed the pint with my compliments easy enough.

Harry   Let them enjoy themselves a while, Iggy. How many of them?

Mush   Six.

Harry   Six.

Mush   There's a rumour one of them is locked up.

Harry   That a pity, Des? Not seven? (*To* **Mush**.) An' yeh?

Mush   The big fella, John –

Iggy   K-k-k-king.'

Harry   Him they call 'The King'.

Mush   Big flat nose.

Iggy   I'll s-s-soon flatten it more for him.

Mush   He's well over forty. (**Harry** *nods*.)

Iggy   I'll – I'll s-s-soon –

Mush   But – Jesus! – I wouldn't like him squeezing my head. He'd give – Jesus! – your ears an awful chewin'. . . .

Harry   Go up and say, right. But that I'm out at the moment, and we're waiting for me, and then we'll be up.

Iggy   N-n-n-no! They'll think we're afraid.

Harry   Naaw. Let them think. They'll think different later. Say nine o'clock we'll be up, Mush, and we'll have a drink, and then ramble up to Rock's Lane.

Mush   Aw, jay, sham –

Harry   Go on.

Mush   Couldn't Hugo go, or –

Harry   No.

Mush *exits.*

Hugo   What about the Killer?

Harry   Naaw. (*Shakes his head at* **Hugo**.)

Hugo   Hah? We could bring him, like, for the crack.

Harry   Naw-naw. (*Winks at* **Hugo**, *nodding behind* **Des**'s *back.*)

Hugo   Hah?

Harry   He's a spoiler! (*To* **Iggy**.) Tucks of time.

Des   What about a plan? Won't we line up in some special way, like in a 'V', maybe?

Harry   None of us goin' writing books of memories later. The best time to think is when you see them across from you. Don't worry, Des, I'll harden your fists. And, Iggy, I have a –

Iggy   I'll m-m-manage without it.

Harry   A handy chain.

Iggy   I'll m-manage without it.

Harry   Five against six, maybe seven.

Iggy   N-n-no one is telling me. I don't have to use none of them things.

Harry   Okay, it's your –

Iggy   M-m-my head.

Harry   Okay.

Iggy   M-m-my head.

Harry   All right.

Iggy   Right.

Harry   Dada?

Dada   No equipment, thank you.

Harry Seems like ye're taking all this like a game. Ah, ye might change yere minds when ye see them. But, person'lly, I'm going to change. Hah? For dinner. I'm not spoiling this jacket. (*Exits and goes upstairs.*)

Iggy Hurry up!

Dada Listen, boys, we all seem to be fixed up all right. Remember, if there's clubs it'll all be over in a few minutes, so get into it right away. Fight for the name, and have valour. And – have valour, and united stand – divided fall. No bickering and – Get into it right away. (*Moves towards door.*) That old factory – Behind that – the one you pointed out to me this morning, Ignatius.

Hugo Where are you going?

Dada There's a little something I'd arranged about this fight tonight.

Hugo But it's at nine –

Dada Nine, yes. Plenty of time to get there if I hurry.

Hugo Where are you going?

Dada A secret, Hubert. My secret. A little surprise I'd arranged for you all. Behind the factory, nine, Rock's Lane, I have that. (*Exits.*)

Iggy (*calls*) Harry!

Hugo (*reflectively*) A surprise he arranged. I wonder what?

Des Dada'll be there.

Iggy Harry!

Hugo Oh, he wouldn't miss it.

Des The waiting is the worst, Iggy? I wish it was over.

Hugo You're not getting afraid, are you?

Iggy Not Des. (*Calls.*) Harry! H-h-harry!

Hugo (*sings*)   'Yummy-yummy-yummy, I've a pain in my tummy.'

Harry (*off, roars*)   Coming! Jesus!

Iggy (*to* **Des**)   I'm always shivery too before anything happens. Shaky, not afraid, just shivery till the second it starts.

Michael *enters. He goes to kitchen door and looks in. He is about to move out of room again.*

Hugo   She's upstairs, rocking the babbies to sleep.

Des   The Mulryans are up in The Lion. (*Pause.*) Six of them. Maybe seven.

Michael   . . . Well, I didn't think ye had that much sense to stay in and keep away from them.

Iggy (*calling* **Harry**)   C-c-come on, sham!

Harry (*off, coming downstairs*)   Tucks of time, tucks of time.

Michael   Surely, ye're not going?

Hugo   We was waiting for you. We love you to jine (*join*) us.

Harry *enters. He has changed into his second-best clothes.*

Harry   Aaa, how yeh, Michael! You got the news?

Michael   I'm surprised Dada isn't here making speeches on this – auspicious, is it? – occasion. I thought it was him I saw hurrying away from the house when I was coming down.

Harry *has been looking around for* **Dada**. *He looks at* **Iggy**. **Iggy** *shrugs. He looks at* **Hugo**.

Hugo   He's gone to get something he forgot. He'll meet us there.

Michael   The next time you'll see him –

Harry   He knows where?

Hugo   Yeh. Dada loves it.

Michael   Take a tip from him and get lost the same.

Harry   Hah? No, Michael. Out to get a few brandies in him he's gone.

Iggy   Are we r-r-right?

Harry   Naaw, let Michael rip. I love being educated by a smart bloke.

Michael   It's no use, Harry. The odds are too big this time. You know about them things. Seven to four now. Seven Mulryans. Not just seven ordinary yahoos just over. And look at all the things they've done in Birmingham for the past ten years. . . . I'm only for your good. . . . Well, have a bit of consideration. You're not taking him (**Des**) with you?

Harry   Yeh?

Michael   I'm only giving you a bit of advice.

Harry   From experience.

Michael   Ye're crazy. That daft father has ye all gone mad. Fighting Carneys! If ye were fighting for a job, even! – A woman, even! Can't you see there's no point. The whole thing is mad, wrong. . . . Well, what if ye win? What does it do for you? Where does it get you? What good is it?

Harry (*stage brogue*)   Oh, 'tis no good at-tall-tall-tall.

Hugo   At-tall-tall-tall.

Michael (*to* **Des**)   You don't have to go. They can't make you.

Harry   Tell him, Des.

Michael   Plain talking now. You can get killed. It's happened before.

Harry   Yeh?

Michael   You might be dead in an hour. Do you know what dead is? Dada wised up. You won't see him again till it's all over . . . Look, the man is as daft, thick and stupid a man as ever lived, but not thick enough to stick his neck out.

Hugo   Why don't you close him up?

Harry   Are you finished, Muscles?

Michael   Tell him what happened in The Bower one night with one of the Mulryans.

Harry   Oh, our kid hears things. You must be mixing with rowdies to be hearing things like that.

Michael   Tell him that.

Hugo   It won't shake Des.

Harry   I'll tell him. Yeh see, Des, one night, 'bout year or two ago, the long-distance Mulryans was up here, and a funny thing happened in The Bower. Some bloke fancied himself, some old eejit, and had a tussle with 'The King' and 'The King' bit off the clown's ear.

Hugo   Half it.

Harry   Mulryan bit off half the clown's ear, and he carries it 'round with him all the time in a matchbox.

Michael   And that's no yarn. That'll tell you what they're like.

Harry   Naw, it's no yarn, but it don't affect our Dessie. I could tell him stories better than that about what we done. He's not like you, pookies. Eh, Dessie?

Michael   Do you want him to finish up like the other Mulryan, the eighth one? – Maybe there were nine of them, but what about the eighth brother? What about him? Tell him that.

Betty *enters.*

Harry What about him? Well, jibber, what about him? Tell the missus, tell sweet Bet-ty, the one that caught you on.

Iggy L-l-let's go.

Harry Naaw!

Hugo Naaw!

Harry Our intelligent brother wants it seven to three. Our intelligent brother is warning him to keep away from us trash. Well, mouth, what about the eighth Mulryan? You tell us.

Michael (*to* **Betty**) Go upstairs.

Harry Stay where you are, English Polly, or whatever your name is. Listen to Tarzan. Michael don't want Polly to see him running like always. After arguments with us he goes back to her and talks all night in bed about how brilliant he was telling us off.

Michael (*to* **Des**) One of the Mulryans was found one morning in a canal. He was only a young lad, just come over. He was all tied up. Ropes and belts and stones on him to weigh him down. The police found him, but they never did anything. They were glad to be rid of him, same as they'd be glad to find you the same way. He was a Mulryan, you're Carney. It's the same thing.

Harry Now, good man, you told him.

Michael Let him talk for himself.

Harry Go on, Des, tell him he's the colour of his daff.

Iggy You're not afraid?

Hugo Tell him.

Des . . . No, I'm going – I'm not afraid of – no one. I never –

Harry Good, Des.

Michael   Give him a chance. Ye don't tell him what to say. Des, look at it –

Harry   Now, Mikey, you're getting more than a chance yourself.

Des (*nervous outburst*)   No. I'm goin'! I'm not afraid of no one! I'm fighting with my brothers! I'm hearing a lot about brothers and helping and that for the last twenty-four hours. They're all against us! We'll get them! (*To* **Michael**.) I think you should be with us too!

Hugo   Bring him, bring him, bring him for the crack!

Harry   If Mikey come he'd be home before us to wet the tea.

Iggy   T-t-too much delaying. Come on, we'll get it over. (*Swaggers out, followed by* **Des** *and* **Hugo**.)

Michael   Des!

Harry (*pushes* **Michael** *back*)   Get out of it, jibber! We'll see you later. Maybe settle our person'l business 'bout the Muslims. Don't forget. And mind English Polly there.

Exits. Pause.

Betty   What are you going to do?

Michael   What do? Aw, you're asking me what am I going to do! What do you think I can do? And what's all this Polly act with you and Harry?

Betty   I can't help it if your brothers are thick.

Michael   Your own family isn't all that nice and respectable.

Betty   Well, they aren't savages or madmen or – If my dad only knew how I was being treated –

Michael   Your dad, your family! If they knew this, if they knew that! I know exactly what your family is like. Like Harry said, I was caught on.

Betty *starts to cry.* **Michael** *is sorry for what he has said. He wants to apologize, to put his arm around her. He can't. Pause.*

Betty   It's no use trying to get them out. We'll have to move ourselves.

Michael   Look at what they're doing to Des.

Betty   It's done – It's done! He's the same as them.

Michael   You don't know him right.

Betty   He isn't worth it. You heard him, afraid of no one. You tried. You only remember him as a child. If he was older than you he'd be the same as the others. (*Pause.*) . . . I don't know. It seems such an easy thing to sit around a table and have a meal.

Michael   Yes, they will.

Betty   *They* won't. Never!

Michael   It's only a stage they're –

Betty   What about last night? 'We'll put him to bed like in the old days.' Does everyone go through that stage? And you had to leave the house.

Michael   I hadn't. I was avoiding trouble.

Betty   Here? Avoid trouble in this place?

Michael   It was their first night over. What did you want to happen?

Betty   You don't owe them anything, Michael.

Michael   I know.

Betty   Well then. You don't have to put up with them.

Michael   I know! I always knew! . . . But they think I do now, since that *stupid* thing happened a few weeks ago. (*She looks at him.*) It's nothing . . . Just, it's on my mind . . . They don't let me forget it anyway. . . . Well, that night my coat was torn that I said I'd fell. I was coming home, and not so far up from here, these four darkies. I was just

passing and one of them pushed me off the path. Said it
was his right-of-way. I didn't say anything. Just started to
go on. And then another one of them stood out in front of
me and started to pull me about. And then I was in the
middle of them, and I started shouting for help. I was in
the middle of them, and they were pushing around,
spitting on me, one of them saying, 'White spit out of black
men.' And I kept shouting for help. And then I saw my
three *thug* brothers running down the road to help me.
Harry first, then Iggy and Hugo. And I saw Iggy
flattening one of them. One blow. They were all fighting.
Mad.

Betty   What happened then?

Michael   I ran . . . It wasn't because I was afraid. I just
don't believe in . . . Oh, God! . . . I stood for a second
watching it all, and then I ran for here . . . That was the
only time in my life I knew my brothers were for me. I
could have been near them that night. But well . . . I don't
know. What's there to do? Harry was in hospital for two
days after that night. I can't go and say, sorry, to Harry
. . . I wasn't afraid. I don't think I'm afraid of anything
either. It was panic.

Betty (*quietly*)   No.

Michael   What?

Betty   No.

Michael   It was –

Betty   What do you want to do?

Michael   What?

Betty   I know you want something. I know I can't give it
to you.

Michael   . . . Oh, that's silly. That's – We're too old for
that kind of talk. . . . Well, I want to get out of all this.
And this awful feeling that something is going to happen
me. I want to get out of this kind of life. I want Des – I

want us all to be – I don't want to be what I am. I want to
read. I don't want to say, 'Yes, sir' to anyone. But I can't
get out of all this. I could have had a good job. I could
have been well fixed. I could have *run* years ago. Away
from them. I could have been a teacher. I had the ability
. . . What's wrong with me? . . .

Betty   You can. You can make more of yourself. And
they'll have more re – (*About to say respect.*) You'll have
more influence over them.

Michael   I know . . . I could've run years ago, but who
would be left with them? Who cared? Not *him*! He's sitting
in some pub now, sucking a brandy, shooting his big
mouth, hiding till this thing is over.

Betty   But what do *you* want to do?

Michael   He's a great help now to his fighting sons.

Betty   But what are you going to do?

Michael   He's a great help to his army.

Betty   But what are you –

Michael   Well, I don't believe in this fighting Carneys. I
don't believe in that game.

Betty   It doesn't matter what you believe at the moment.
You owe them something – you said it yourself. Don't start
bringing you father or –

Michael   What?

Betty   I'm only trying to tell you stop and think for a
moment. It's no good going from one thing to the other.

Michael   I'll do the deciding about what's good and bad.

Betty   Ah, I'm sick! You come crying your stories to me,
and I listen –

Michael   No one is asking you to –

Betty   I'm sick to death! First Iggy, then Harry, then your father, then Des! – Des! – Des! And then you want something, and then you owe them something. I go to talk and I'm told to shut up. You won't put them out, you won't leave – what are you going to do?

Michael   What do you want me to do?

Betty   Fight!

Michael   Fight! You know how I feel about –

Betty   Fight! Fight! Fight! Do something! Fight anything! And then maybe we can –

Michael   And won't that prove –

Betty   Don't start it all over again –

Michael   But wouldn't that prove to them after all my years' talking against it that –

Betty   Fight! They'll think more of you. Respect you. I'll think more of you. If that matters any more. We'll do something then. We'll go. Or they'll go. We'll have a better chance if you prove you're not a . . .

Michael (*quietly, simply*)   What? . . . Finish it.

Betty (*crying*)   I don't know what's happening, love.

Michael (*quietly*)   Jesus! . . . Jesus! . . . Prove I'm not a coward. (*Grabs a milk bottle.*) With a milk bottle, is it? Blood, and fighting, and light-heads, and daft fathers, and mad brothers! With this is it? (*Throws the bottle away and grabs a knife.*) Or this? Hah? Do you want me to use it? Hah? (*Throws the knife away.*) Right. Right then. I'm Carney too, another Carney. Right.

Michael *exits.* **Betty** *cries quietly.*

Act Three

A few hours later, **Dada** *is sitting at the table. He is drunk. A small 'elastoplast' (Band-Aid) on his forehead. On the table, two bottles of whiskey, cups, glasses and a small parcel. Through the following, he sings snatches of 'I hear You Calling Me'.*

Betty *is standing at the front door, looking out. She moves in and out to the front door during the scene.*

Dada (*singing*) 'I hear you calling me; you called me when the moon had veiled her light; before I went from you into the night, you spoke . . .' Beautiful song that. Not many can sing it. Lovely. 'Still here's the distant music of your voice'. . . . No use going in and out like that, ma'am. Relax. Take deep breaths. Deep breaths is the secret. Look. (*Inhales and exhales, admiring his chest expansion.*) See that? Now I'm completely relaxed. Whiskey helps too. It relaxes the throat, the muscles. You have muscles in your throat, you know . . . Yeah. All great singers have a couple of half-ones before they go out. You get the high notes then. (*Drinks, clears his throat, sings.*) 'I hear you calling me.' . . . Lovely . . . Try a drop, ma'am? Put a bit of life in you. It's food, you know. No? Barley and rye and things. (*Raises his glass.*) As my brother, Father Kevin, used to say – Did Michael tell you I've a brother a priest, the foreign missions? . . . No? Well, I have! . . . As he used to say – (*Raises his glass again.*) *Humanum est errare*, there is truth in wine! (*Drinks. Pause.*) . . . Do you ever feel lonely? . . . I always thought I'd have a house with nice music. . . . Wha'?

Betty You could go out and look for them.

Dada Don't worry, ma'am. Cross your bridges – when they come to you. (*Laughs.*) . . . Yeah . . . Any books in the house, good books?

Betty No.

Dada   Wha'? . . . None at all?

Betty   No.

Dada   Doesn't he read? It's education to read. This wouldn't be my house. At home I've two rooms full of books. Valuable. Worth a thousand – more – a few thousand pounds. Wouldn't sell them. I have! They can't be got at all now. Did you ever read *The History of Ancient Greece*, did you? I'm reading that now, just before I came over. Very interesting on how . . . Yeh. Did you ever read *True Men As We Need Them?* . . . No . . . I bet you never read *Ulysses?* Hah? – Wha'? – Did you? No. A Dublin lad and all wrote *Ulysses*. Great book. Famous book. All about how . . . how . . . Yeah . . . Can't be got at all now. All classic books like them I have. No Buck Jones stuff for me . . . He used to read one time. Doesn't he now?

Betty   No.

Dada   No . . . Do you think he's intelligent?

Betty   No – Yes.

Dada   Do you?

Betty   I do.

Dada   Well, I don't . . . He doesn't read, you said! Like, he – Well, he isn't a good conversationalist. Like, well he – Well, there's more caffeine in tea than coffee. Caffeine, the drug, you know. (*Pause.*) . . . You were a clerk once, weren't you? . . . Michael said you were . . . Nice clean job . . . Did he ever tell you I was a guard once? Did he ever tell you I was a guard, a policeman?

Betty   No.

Dada   No. He wouldn't. No . . . Well, I was! . . . A lot of clerical work attached to that . . . But they – No, I didn't like it anyway. Packed it in. I resigned! . . . Does he be talking about me?

Betty   He never talks about you at all.

Dada N-a-a-a-w! . . . He thinks he knows it all. But he doesn't know much about life. Very smart. Very – very – very smart. (*Drinks, pauses, sings.*) . . . 'Do you remember me standing there? For one last kiss, beneath the kind stars' light.' (*Drinks, pause. Suddenly.*) . . . I hate! I hate the world! It all! . . . But I'll get them! I'll get them! By the sweet, living, and holy Virgin Mary, I'll shatter them! They accepted me. They drank with me. I made good conversation. Then, at their whim, a little pip-squeak of an architect can come along and offer me the job as caretaker. To clean up after him! But I'll – I'll – Do you hear me? I hate! . . . (*Grows softer.*) Oh, I wish to God I was out of it all. I wish I had something, anything. Away, away, some place. . . . No. No! I'm proud. I did all right by my family. Didn't I? . . . Yaas! (*Passionately to himself.*) On my solemn oath I did my best . . . My best, my best, my best. I'm proud of them. Yah – yah – yah! I hate! (*Looks up and sees* **Betty** *watching him. Softly.*) . . . Sit down, ma'am, can't you. Do you ever feel lonely?

Betty Michael talks like that sometimes when he –

Dada Aw, Michael – Michael – Michael! Is that all you can say? Did he tell you not to listen to me? I talk through my hat?

Betty No.

Dada You think he's great, don't you?

Betty Yes, I think – I –

Dada Oh, don't mind me. I'm daft, stupid. But you think he's great.

Betty Yes. Yes! I do!

Dada Well, he's only a shit! Now do you know? Do you know now? That's what he is!

Betty *goes out to front door. Men's voices off.* **Dada** *pulls himself together and goes out to the door to meet his sons.* **Iggy, Des, Hugo, Mush** *and* **Harry** *enter,* **Des** *swaggering like* **Iggy**.

They carry marks of the fight – nothing extreme. **Mush** *possibly, looking the worst; pale and shaken.*

Dada ⎱   Ah-haa! . . . Ah –
Betty ⎰   Where's Michael? . . . Where's Michael? . . .

Des   (*We*) Slaughtered them.

Dada   No need to ask how it went! Aha! No better men!

Betty   What did you do with him?

Hugo   Your man's face after the chain.

Dada   Ah-haa! I have the drinks laid in. Come on.

Betty   Where is he, Des?

Des   Don't be annoying me. Dada, Iggy made a right job of 'The King'.

Dada   Man, Ignatius! Drinks, boys!

Hugo   Mush wasn't supposed to be in it at all, but he got in the way of . . . (*They laugh.*)

Mush (*pushes his chin out at* **Harry**)   Here, break your fist off that and report yourself sick. (*They laugh.*)

Iggy   They wasn't expecting the chain.

Des   And, Dada, I got this fella such a clout –

Hugo   When the fight was over, Des gave one little bloke, that was just standing watching, a terrible dig in the head.

Des   He's roaring yet.

Iggy   Naw, they wasn't expecting the chain.

Des   Aw, but did ye see the way the crowd pulled back to let us out? A kind of silence, fright, respect, they had.

Hugo   There was no one making passageway to let out the Mulryans.

Iggy   They wasn't expecting the chain. It's not the same winning that way.

Des Naw, Iggy, naw. We won. We got revenge for you, Mush, didn't we?

Hugo Aw, Jays, Mush moving across, just before it began, and Mulryan drew out – (*They laugh.*)

Mush I was going to – (*The laughter drowns him.*)

Dada Good man, Mush.

Mush Well, the last fella I hit, I hit him such a blow that he used fall at the same time every night for a fortnight. (*They laugh.*)

Harry Have a drink, Betty. Come on, jine us.

Betty Where is he, Harry? He went out right after you, to help you.

Des I seen him, Betty. There he was in the middle of it, flattening all round him.

Harry (*to* **Betty**) Yeh? Went out? That so? (*To the others.*) Hear that? (*To* **Betty**.) You wouldn't be making things up now, like, so we'd be nice to him?

Hugo You couldn't be up to Bitchey. Ye're well met, Michael and yourself.

Harry But come on, Betty, jine us.

Hugo He's a traitor, that's what he is. Isn't he, Dada?

Dada Drink up, boys. In with the Mulryans, that's the place you'd find him.

Betty And where were you tonight?

Dada . . . What do you mean?

Betty Did you help them?

Dada Oh, this is serious now, ma'am. I see. My fidelity is in doubt. Where was I? Is that your question? Boys? . . . You see, my sons, my own haven't the audacity, but I must answer you, a stranger. And a stranger I know nothing about!

Hugo   She has no right − (**Dada** *silences him.*)

Betty   All I want to know is where is he. He did, really, go out after you.

Des   Maybe he did.

Harry   What?

Des   Michael?

Harry   Out to fight with − ? Michael won't hardly mix with us outside. He's a big shot, good boy, messenger boy.

Dada   Correct, Henry.

Des   Naw. You're wrong.

Harry   Are you telling me?

Des   You have to think these things out. You see, with Michael −

Harry   You're explaining to me?

Dada   Desmond, Michael looks on us −

Harry   Stall now a minute. He's going *explaining* to me.

Dada   I'll explain.

Harry   Hah? *You're* explaining too?

Dada   Henry, I said −

Harry   No-no-no-no. He's going to tell me how I can't think things out.

Dada   It's bad manners to interrupt.

Harry (*considers for a moment*)   . . . Right. Just one question of you so first. Just one −

Dada   Desmond·is under the misconception −

Harry   Desmond is under a lot of things, but one question of you first. Like she said, where were you?

Betty *goes out to the front door.*

Dada   . . . Do I –

Harry   *I'd* love to know.

Dada   Well, I'm coming to it, Henry. . . . Gentlemen, we are having a dual celebration tonight. Not just one victory, but for my victory too. . . . Yes! (*Taps the Band-Aid on his forehead.*) Ah-haa, ye weren't the only battlers! You know wild horses wouldn't have kept me from the Mulryans tonight.

Hugo   Did something happen?

Dada   Did something happen? Wait'll you hear. Remember when I left here tonight?

Harry   I was upstairs.

Dada   Well, Henry, I hit for a certain place to get this. (*Takes up the small parcel off the table.*) The surprise, Hubert. And then I said I'd have two drinks – Now, only two, mind – in the – what's this you call the pub? The – The – Oh, it doesn't matter. I got this little batch of stuff there too. (*The whiskey.*) I came out, and I was making my way for Rock's Lane, and I got a bit lost for a while. But don't mind that so much. Anyway, I found myself in this darkish laneway, and all of a sudden, there's a fella stepping out in front of me, out of nowhere. Out of nowhere, he's beside me. 'Got a light, mate?' he says, kind of sizing me up. I suppose I look the wealthy type. 'Sorry,' I said. I was out before, you know. 'Got a fag?' he said then, still in front of me. 'Out of the way,' I said, pushing him out of my way. Then I saw this other fella hurrying towards me, and I heard a noise behind, and wasn't there a third guy sloping up on me as well.

Des   Like the Mulryan fella tonight when –

Iggy   Three of them, was it?

Hugo   Quares, was it?

Dada   Makes no matter what they were or wanted, but they were out for me, and I knew it.

Hugo   Yeh?

Iggy   Maybe someone we had a tangle with and they knew you.

Dada   I thought of that, Ignatius. But, anyway – Henry – I got my back to the wall and it started. Ah-haa, there's power in the old man yet! The first fella seemed to go mad when he saw I wasn't going to take it sitting-down style. He charged at me – Oh, a right lunatic! 'I'll swing for you!' he shouted.

Hugo   What did you do?

Dada   I swung for him! (*They laugh.*)

Iggy   Did she go down?

Dada   Like a sack. He didn't get up neither.

Des   Where was all this?

Dada   The other two came at me. I got a right one here in the jaw. Still sore. I thought I was gone. It isn't swelled, is it?

Hugo   Naw-naw – Go on, Dada.

Dada   And a right one in the forehead. I thought the plaster would help. Ah, it didn't really need it. Just a bruise.

Iggy   The other two. What did –

Dada   You see, one of them made this kick at me, and I part ducked it. But I said then, all right, if that's the way ye want it. And I lashed and kicked and kicked and lashed. I suppose the same was happening to me, but I never felt it.

Iggy   Aw.

Dada   But I put the second fella across the road, he hit the wall, and down.

Iggy   Did you put the three of them away?

Dada   No. No. I was nearly away myself. After the second fella I got this kick, right here. (*Feels his groin.*) And lucky thing for me, the third guy wasn't too anxious 'cause I was bunched. Anyone'd be. And the pain, and winded, you know. And I started to get away quick as I could, and when I got to the main street, I had to throw myself on a seat there. Lord, I was bad, but I didn't care who was looking. Sick as a dog, bunched completely, not worth two-pence. And I couldn't stir, I'm telling you. Not for hours . . . I'm not as young as I was, boys.

Hugo   Talking about a night!

Dada   But I knew ye wouldn't let me down. The Carneys for it!

Hugo   Three of them! God! I'd love to have seen you in action. And that little bitch out there was on to you. And when we should have been with you. (*Calls.*) Hey! Hey, you! Asking where he was. Come here if you want to know!

Dada (*unwrapping the parcel*)   Leave her; she's not worth it.

Hugo (*shouts*)   Dada always has a good excuse!

Dada   I'd arranged in my mind to get this. A little surprise. (*The parcels contains a small silver-plated cup.*) What do ye think of that? That's what I had arranged to get.

Hugo   Lord, it's the real thing.

Dada   A gesture.

Des   Show it here.

Mush   Smashing.

Dada   Gesture.

Hugo   That's valuable.

Iggy   Aw.

Dada   Don't mind the cost. Only the best is good enough. That's silver. Give it to me. We'll do this right. Henry. I'll present it proper. Properly. I present ye, Carneys, with this cup – trophy – magnificent trophy – for your courage and bravery in the face of the enemy. Outstanding. Ye fought bravely and well, and with indomitable courage – indomitable courage, and ye – ye fought bravely and well. Ye kept the flag flying high and ye – ye fought bravely and well. Here, you take it, Henry. I present it to you (**Dada** *and* **Harry** *are looking at each other*.) . . . The captain – the general . . . A gesture from an old man.

After another moment, **Harry** *accepts it silently.*

Dada   Congratulations! Good man, Henry! Great lads! Aw, ye're great lads! I'm proud of ye! Champions of England! Great Irishmen! The Carney name will be known all over! Stout-hearted men!

Mush   From the County Mayo.

Iggy   Aw.

Hugo   Give us that one, Dada.

Dada (*false reluctance*)   Aw, no.

Mush   Go on, Mr Carney, a song.

Dada   Aw no.

Hugo   We'll make a right party out of it. You give us a song, Mush.

Harry   One of your own make-ups, Mush.

Hugo   The one about Harry.

Mush   I've a new one wrote.

Des   Who about?

Mush   Iggy. Will I give it?

Hugo   In t'it.

Harry   Silence now. One voice and one voice only.

Mush (*produces a slip of paper and recites*)
    Iggy the Iron Man.

I knew a great big noble man,
His name was Iggy Carney;
He was big and strong, could sing a song
Could –

Hugo Iggy can't sing.

Iggy Shush!

Harry On, Mush.

Mush He was big and strong, could sing a song,
Could lift the stone of Blarney;
His hands was big and hard and swift,
They really were quite mighty;
And them that stood again' that bloke
Was soon put out of sighty.

When Iggy crossed the Atlantic foam
To England's foggy dew,
His name had swam before him
And all the tough-uns drew;
They tried to take his crown from him
But in the end they ran,
The hair oil scalding their cut-up heads,
Away from the Iron Man.

Oh, Iron Man, Oh Iron Man, we proudly sing thy name;
If Brian Boru let us down, thou kept up Erin's fame;
Thou beat and blackened men galore for the sake of
    liberty,
From the dear old glens in sweet Mayo
To the shores round Coventry.

Mush *is applauded. They cheer and laugh.*

Hugo Good man, Mush!

Harry Give him another pint and fire him out!

Through the applause **Dada** *is standing in a corner with his back to
them. He starts to sing. The noise subsiding, and they listen with
considerable reverence.*

Dada (*sings 'The Boys from the County Mayo'*)
  Far away from the land of the shamrock and heather,
  In search of a living as exiles we roam,
  And whenever we chance to assemble together,
  We think of the land where we once had a home.
  But those homes are destroyed and our land confiscated,
  The hand of the tyrant brought plunder and woe;
  The fires are now dead and our hearths desolated,
  In our once happy homes in the County Mayo.
    (*Chorus.*)
  So, boys, stick together in all kinds of weather,
  Don't show the white feather wherever you go;
  Be each as a brother and love one another,
  Like stout-hearted men from the County Mayo.

Dada *is applauded.*

If only I had accompaniment, piano.

Harry   Quiet now again for Mush.

Hugo   A song now, Mush.

Mush   Aw, don't be asking me after a singer like your father.

Dada   Try something anyway, it doesn't have to be as good.

Iggy   Naw, give's 'Harry from the Land of Saints and Scholars.'

Des   Is there none about me?

Mush   No, I'll sing –

Des   Seems like you've them all about the others.

Harry   Ary, don't mind him. Give 'Harry from the Land of –

Dada   Gentlemen! I propose we drink a toast. We'll drink to ourselves, the Carneys, on this memorable and momentous victory over the Mulryans, on this historic day – night – the twenty-fourth ult., nineteen hundred and –

Mush   Inst.

Hugo   Hah?

Mush   You shoud've said inst., not ult.

Dada   Mr O'Reilly is trying to tell me, boys, that I should have said inst. instead of ult. People, instead of saying the name of the month, for short they say –

Mush   Inst.

Dada   Ult.

Hugo   Ult! Ult!

Mush   No, he should've said –

Des   Close it! (*Your mouth.*)

Hugo   Ult!

Mush   Hah? (*Nervously.*) Hah-haa!

Des   You might be able to fool the others a bit, but not me. (*Looks round to see if the rest of the family is watching him.*) What do you mean, anyway, interrupting?

Mush   I was only trying to –

Des (*hits* **Mush**)   Well, don't be 'onlyin',' d'yeh hear?

Harry (*advising* **Mush**)   Cobblers, Mush. Lesson number two.

Dada, **Iggy** *and* **Hugo** *are laughing.* **Des** *laughs and starts to pursue* **Mush**. **Mush** *bolts for the door and escapes,* **Des** *missing him with a kick as he exits.*

Mush (*off*)   Tinkers! Carneys! Tinkers! Tinkers!

Des *grabs a whiskey bottle and dashes out after* **Mush**. *He is heard breaking the bottle outside.*

Iggy (*to* **Harry** *who remains motionless*)   Let it go, sham. (*Calls after* **Des**.) Come back! Des! (*To the others.*) Mush'd bring the police awful fast. She's a terror for the shades when she's in trouble.

Dada (*laughs*)   I was sure he'd be another Michael. Him and Michael when they were small, ye know –

Harry   And when they was big too.

Des *enters, broken bottle in his hand.*

Iggy   Did you get her?

Des   Naw.

Dada   Good man, Desmond! He's nearly soused. He learns fast, doesn't he?

Des   Learning! (*Tapping his head.*) Up here you want it.

Harry   There was still some –

Des (*pointing at his feet*)   Down there for dancing.

Harry (*tapping his head*) Up here in your arse. There was still some whiskey left in that bottle.

Des   Ho-ho, learning! Anyone care to try me? Anyone? Anyone that likes? Any time?

Hugo (*laughs*)   Any place.

Des   What are you laughing at? Do you think I wouldn't take you?

Hugo (*laughs*)   I'm bloody sure of it.

Des   You stupid get!

Hugo (*jumps up.* **Iggy** *moves in between them*)   Are you starting the superior game now? I'll burst your big head in. I'll make him sorry he ever came.

Iggy (*easing the bottle from* **Des**)   Sit down, the two of ye. I thought we were celebrating.

Des   I did more than him in the fight, didn't I?

Iggy   Sit down, Des.

Des   Didn't you see the state I left your man in?

Iggy   We seen it.

Hugo   Let him go, and see the state I'll leave him in.

Harry (*quietly*)   Let them at it.

Hugo   Nobody is calling me a – names.

Iggy (*to* **Hugo**)   Sit down. She's drunk.

Hugo *sits.* **Des** *gets cocky again.*

Des   Maybe you fancy yourself too, hah?

Iggy   Naw. (*Winks at* **Hugo**.) You'd take any of us.

Des   Well, like I said now, any of ye that wants it. (*About to sit, changes his mind. Then, into* **Iggy**'s *face.*) Well, Iron M-m-m-man?

Split-second pause, then **Iggy** *sweeps* **Des** *back against the wall and is up against him with amazing speed.* **Des** *flinches.*

Iggy   No more now. You shut up when I say to, or you'll have no mouth. Do you understand that? (*Short pause. Then* **Harry** *laughs at* **Des**.) A sing-song! 'So-s-so, boys, stick together in all kinds of weather, don't show the white feather wherever you go. Be each . . .' (*Etc.*)

The others join in; **Dada** *providing a strange counterpoint with his Irish tenor 'Oft in the Stilly Night'. Through this,* **Michael** *has come in front door. He is drunk.* **Betty** *has tried to persuade him not to join the party. He enters the room, followed by* **Betty**. *He stands there for a few moments before they notice him.*

Hugo   Look!

Harry   We won, Michael, you'll love to hear!

Iggy   I wonder had she much to drink?

Harry   Ten points while the Angelus was ringin'. Give us an auld warble, Michael.

Dada (*sings*)   'Oft in the Stilly Night, ere slumber chains have . . .'

Hugo   Give her a drink.

Harry   Sing for Des. You like Des.

Hugo   Sing for Betty.

Harry   Poor disappointed Polly – (*To* **Betty**.) Keep out of it, English Polly! We won, Michael, you'll love to hear. But we just want you to know we just turned over a new leaf. And we come to the conclusion that Des is going back to Mary Horan's country. And Hugo is going to the university, and I'm going paying for his fees. And Iggy is going joining the Foreign Legion of Mary. And Dada is going off, with his old one-two, killing communists. And I'm going joining the nuns.

Betty   Let's go upstairs, Michael.

Harry   No-no-no-no-no, wait'll you hear –

Betty   We don't want to hear!

Dada   Don't be unsociable, ma'am.

Betty   We've heard enough.

Hugo (*giggles*)   Upstairs.

Dada (*sings*)   'Sad memory brings the light of other days around me . . .'

Betty   Come on, love. (**Michael** *pushes her hand away*.)

Harry   See what I mean? That's what I was going to say. He's a killer at heart. Ask any of the lads. Even when we was small –

Hugo } World Champ Carney –
Harry } Do you know what he'd be at, Polly? Off
    strangling asses in the morning before his
    breakfast. Just for practice. Yeh. That's right.
    And he'd be –

Betty   Stop it! Stop it! We don't want to hear any more.

Harry   But we just want some more advice.

Betty   You're not funny!

Harry   She don't understand, Michael! Look, we have a party in the family. Our victory. What do you say? Look: happy family, brothers stickin' together in all kinds of weather.

Dada   Don't show the white feather –

Harry   Michael never shown that.

Dada   No.

Hugo   No.

Dada   Ignatius?

Iggy   Aw.

Dada   Desmond?

Des   Well, maybe we should –

Harry   Yeh?

Des   Like, well, make it up now. Like, it would –

Harry   Yeh? . . . Like? . . . But person'lly, I wouldn't like to tangle with the ass-strangler.

Michael (*drunkenly, smiling, to himself*)   This is your victory party?

Harry   Shh-shh-shh-shh, the advice is coming. Yeh? (**Michael** *shakes his head, muttering to himself*.) . . . Hah?

Betty   Come on, Michael.

Michael (*smiling*)   Who are you coddin'? Your victory party.

Harry   Hah?

Betty   Leave it, Michael.

Harry   Hah?

Betty   Come on, Michael.

Harry   No, I don't think he's saying congratulations –

Betty   Stop it!

Michael   Is this your victory party over *them*?

Harry   No, I don't think he's saying well done. I don't think he's —

Betty   Stop it!

Michael   Over *them*?

Dada   See him sneering? Don't take it off him.

Harry (*to* **Michael**)   Hah?

Betty   Stop it! Stop it! Stop it! You all must get out of here now! You must! Now! We don't care where you go! You must leave us! All of you.

Michael   Keep out of it.

Dada   Who's talking? The woman? The stranger?

Harry   No, Michael is going to throw me out.

Betty   We've had enough!

Hugo   Aaa, Betty me love — (*Pushes her on top of* **Michael**.) Michael is going to throw me out.

Betty   Pigs! Pigs! You're only pigs! Animals! That's all you are. (*Takes* **Michael***'s arm. He pulls free of her.*)

Harry   Yis?

Michael (*to* **Betty**)   No, you don't belong to this great victory party over *them*.

Dada   What's he saying?

Betty (*to* **Dada**)   You should have more sense, than having them go on like this.

Dada   Ha-haa, boys!

Michael (*to* **Betty**)   Go upstairs.

Harry   Yis?

Hugo (*giggling*) Upstairs.

Michael And fester all night over *them*. And if you can do that, you'll be allowed join in the next victory party we have over *them*.

Betty Come on, love, please. (*She is tugging at his arm.*)

Dada Listen to him, boys.

Hugo (*giggling*) Love. Love.

Betty And if you don't go – If you're not gone in the morning – We'll – We'll have you out. We'll –

Michael I said keep out of it.

Harry Yis-yis-yis?

Betty We'll call the police.

Michael I said keep out of it.

Harry Yis-yis-yis?

Betty Please, Michael, please, love, come on, please . . .

Harry Yis-yis-yis? (**Michael** *pulls his arm free, and hits her. Triumphantly.*) Yis!

Michael *and* **Betty** *stand looking at each other. The others are laughing.* **Betty** *exits upstairs.*

Dada Ha-haa, boys!

Michael You dirty hypocrite.

Dada First, he nearly threw us all out; then, he hit the poor little missus.

Michael (*quietly*) The years I saw how you treated Mama. (*They continue laughing, refilling their glasses, etc.* **Michael** *watching them. Quietly.*) Your poor, big, stupid mouths.

Iggy Aa, who a-a-are – do you think you're talking to?

Michael All your poor, big, stupid, ignorant mouths.

Iggy   You didn't get so far with all your clever ways!

Harry (*first realization*)   Hah? That's right!

Dada (*first realization*)   That's right! Good lads!

Harry   All his big talk and he's no bank manager nowhere.

Dada   He didn't do so well after all, did he? No!

Michael   If I had –

Harry   Aa, Mikey boy, if-if-if! If you got a chance, is it?

Iggy   Give her another chance to hit Betty again.

Harry   If your head wasn't so big, is it?

Michael   If I could have got away from ye!

Harry   If you weren't so handsome, like. All them other managers got the breaks, 'cept you.

Dada   If Hugo got a chance he'd be a scientist, making –

Hugo   Bombs, Dada, bombs!

Harry   Now, I find that very interesting about you. And poor Des got no chance neither. Only for us he would. Tough that.

Michael (*goes to* **Harry**)   If I had got away from things like ye!

Dada   Don't take it off him, Henry –

Harry   Stall. (*To* **Michael**.) What?

Michael   Anything else to say tonight? . . . Anything else to do?

Harry   Hah?

Michael   To make you happy. To get it all off your chest.

Harry   . . . Ah . . . yeh. Yeh. I agree with you about everything. You're real intelligent and I'm not, and you're always right, and I like that. Even about Mush and things.

And I agree you'd never see a fella stuck, like, old stock.
And the evening you were passing with some respectable
bird one time, and I was standing outside the cinema, and
I don't think you mustn't have seen me at first 'cause your
eyes just flickered and you walked right past and didn't say
hello. But then – I didn't understand it. But I feel a few
other lads standing round the cinema did, 'cause they
smiled. And you said to her, ''scuse me', and you come
back to me, sort of serious stranger, never said a word,
slipped me a tanner, so I could go in and be hid from view.
Remember that?

Michael   Anything else?

Harry   Hah? . . . Yeh. I 'preciated that favour. And
you'd never run, say, if your old buddies was fighting for
you, like. Hah? Isn't that it? That's it. Yeh. Pals. (*Turns
away from* **Michael**. *Then he turns back, his fists clenched to hit*
Michael. **Michael** *has expected this, and stands with his hands
at his sides.* **Harry** *pauses momentarily, then punches* **Michael** *in
the stomach.* **Michael** *slumps to the floor.*) Isn't that it! – Isn't
that it! – Isn't that it!

Michael   God, ye're so – so – so –

Harry   Thick! (*Kicking* **Michael**.)

Michael   Thick!

Dada   Do ye hear him, lads?

Harry   Yes, we're so thick, stupid, twisted, thick! Oh,
Michael, you are such a bright boy.

Dada   Haha-haa! The bright boy! Look at him now!

Harry (*turns on* **Dada**)   But that's what you think, isn't it?
All us others in the family was thick, but he was bright boy.

Dada   I never – No, never said that, Henry.

Harry   But you thought it.

Dada   Me? Him? I thought him intelligent?

Harry   Yes, yes, yeh, you! You never said it, but it was there.

Dada   But-but-but, he's the flop in the house.

Harry (*a plea*)   But mean it, mean it!

Des   Michael got a better education, Harry, than –

Harry   If I say a thing I'll mean it, I'll fight for it. No old crap talk, nor not knowing where I stand, nor –

Dada   Yes, he's no bank manager, Henry. He's no –

Harry (*to* **Dada**)   Or 'little surprises' from others. (*The silver cup.*)

Des   Michael was two years at the secondary school in –

Harry   Keep quiet, you, I'm not so keen on you neither. Person'lly, I don't mind a man, no matter what he talks, if he means it, and you can see it, and if he'll stand up for it, and if he's – faithful.

Des   I was only pointing out –

Harry   What's the money doing in your top pocket? (**Des**'*s hand goes to his top pocket.*)

Hugo   He made out he'd none tonight when we was buying.

Harry   That's all right – that's all right.

Des   I didn't want you to think that I –

Dada   Money, Henry? Where did he get it?

Harry   I know where he got it. That doesn't matter. Faithful. I could admire he saying he's no money. It's the other – the – the other things – the – the –

Dada   Implications, Henry.

Harry   Things! He doesn't think we can think straight. The things that's behind him. The things – where does he stand? Getting fed two sides, like. The sort of – the – the –

Dada   Implications.

Harry   *Things!* (*He kicks a chair.*)

Dada   I understand –

Harry   No.

Dada   I –

Harry   No.

Dada   Actions have roots, I can explain.

Harry   No! Not to me. No explaining to me. Things are clear enough to me. There's been so many good intelligent blokes for so long explaining things to thick lads. So many. So worried. All them clever blokes, cat smart, so worried about it all. (*Points at* **Michael**.) He's so big and bright, he talks about families and home and all, and he's ashamed of us. See him apologizing to Betty when he invited us here. Little jokes for all, so she could take us. And all the time he doesn't know me outside. The preacher. Family. Home. (**Harry** *is suppressing tears.*) But I'm thick. Thick lads don't feel, they can't be offended.

Michael *pulls himself up off the floor.*

Dada   Yes, yas, yas, that's him all right! That's –

Harry   No! Not *you*! I'm talking now. (*To* **Michael**.) You worry about me, don't you? And then you apologize to them with the lovely white collars for me, don't you? And to them with the lovely white collars you say, 'Yes, sir, I'm a pig, sir, if you say so, sir!' And be pleased, 'cause they're surprised, smile to you, your manners, a pat on the head to a dog. And then you're better'n me?

Dada   Yes, Henry, no pride. He'll bow and scrape, and –

Harry   I'm talking. (*To* **Michael**.) Yes! You're right there too! I did salute McQuaide once. But I'm not still tearing the head off myself, pulling off my cap to salute them shams. They kick, you salute, and then they pray for you. Pray for the poor dirty pigs over here, now and at the hour of our death.

Dada   Amen.

Hugo   Amen.

Harry   . . . Amen.

Dada   Ignatius?

Iggy (*quietly*)   I know what's he's talking about.

Pause.

Des   Oh, I don't know. (*Wanting to assert himself.*)

Harry   Yeh?

Pause.

Michael (*to* **Harry**)   Anything else?

Dada   Look! He's still better than us.

Michael (*to* **Dada**)   I thought you made all the speeches?

Dada   My authority – My authority is – I endorse all Henry said. (*Viciously.*) I'll settle you yet.

Michael (*to* **Harry**)   Are you happy now?

Des   Oh, I don't know. I'm not a fool around here. All this talk is inferiority –

Harry   Aaa, inferior complex. I know about that one too. That's a very handy one always when any of us, the thick lads, says anything about the big nobs – crap faces.

Des   Not inferior complex; it's an inferiority complex.

Harry   Hah?

Dada   Inferiority complex, Henry, that's right.

Harry (*glances at* **Dada***; then to* **Des**)   You're another almost terribly brainy bloke. You explain to me too. Aa, but you're wider than Tarzan here. You wear the sure-

I'm-only-a-young-lad-foolish-but-there's-no-harm-in-me look. You like my nouns-'n'singulars?

Des I – They – I – Hah? (*Starts to sway drunkenly.*)

Harry No-no-no-no-no-no-no-no-no now! Don't gam on drunk. That's another special act with some. Drunk, like. No one is ever drunk till he's out, out cold. Funny, a thick lad like me knowing them things. You like the ways I talk?

Des Why?

Harry Hah now. I'm asking you.

Des It's all the same to me how you talk.

Harry Hah? I like the ways I talk too. (*Laughs.*) You're not so drunk now, are you? I like the ways our Michael talks too. He's not drunk neither now. I think he should have been our daddy, I think he should have you then, 'cause he wants to look after you so much, and you like him. (*Pushes* **Des** *across at* **Michael**.)

Des (*trying to laugh it off*) Aw, easy, Harry, Harry sham, easy.

Harry (*pushes* **Des** *back at* **Michael** *again*) Naw. But you're frightened now, not drunk. That's funny. You frightened too, Michael?

Michael Yes.

Harry (*to* **Iggy** *and* **Hugo**) Look at them!

Michael Anything else?

Harry (*smiles, shakes his head*) No. I'm happy now.

Harry, **Iggy** *and* **Hugo** *are on one side of the stage,* **Michael**, **Dada** *and* **Des** *on the other.* **Harry**, **Iggy** *and* **Hugo** *are refilling their glasses.* **Hugo** *is looking for beer.* **Harry** *is croaking to himself – non-singing voice – 'So, boys, stick together . . .' etc.* **Michael** *starts to walk out of the room.*

Dada Wait! Wait! Wait, you! Henry! Henry! Boys! . . . (*They all look around at him and find him standing on a chair.*

Dada *is also trying to reassert himself. Now that he has got their attention he does not know what to say. Trying to think of something to say.*) . . . Ah-haa! . . . Ah-haa for the Carneys! No better men! (**Michael** *starts to move off again.*) Wait! Wait, you! . . . Boys! . . . Boys, boys . . . World Champ Carney! Clear the room, furniture back! Wait, you!

Michael   For Christ's sake!

Dada   Like in the old days. See who's the best man, Desmond.

Harry   Or maybe, us three again' ye three?

Dada   All must obey me now. My authority. My authority. Orders. Abide by the rules, Henry. Get that chair back against the wall, Hubert.

Hugo   World Champ Carney!

Michael   How come you were always referee?

Dada   Getting brazen again. Soon fix that. Referee – procedure – authority – has to be referee. You should remember this game well, Michael.

Michael   For Christ's sake! And ye're all getting out of here in the morning!

Dada   Watch your language before me, boy.

Harry (*laughs*)   The three of them again' themselves.

Dada   Thank God, boys, I could always stand up and –

Michael   Hit, belt, clout –

Dada   Yes!

Michael   Children! Hit kids!

Dada   Could always stand up, boys, talk with the best.

Michael   Hit children!

Dada   Never bad language, never swore.

Michael   Coming home, vomiting brandy and porter.

Dada   Hasn't learned his lesson yet. Come on, boys –

Michael   In a temper, sulking, after his conversations with the big-shot friends. 'We'll get them!'

Dada   No change in him.

Michael   Pulling four little kids out of bed, two, three, four in the morning. And up on a chair. 'World Champ Carney! Ah-haa for the Carneys! We'll get them! Charge!' And we all belted into one another.

Dada   Three of ye! Three!

Michael   And you still see nothing wrong with that?

Dada   But little Michael – our eldest, boys –

Michael   And there's nothing wrong with this now?

Dada   Our eldest, boys, remember? Wouldn't fight!

Michael   A ridiculous old man, still roaring on the chair!

Dada   Wouldn't fight! Ashamed of him! Dribbling, whimpering, like a mangy dog in a corner!

Michael   What's wrong with you? Why always the –

Dada   Nothing wrong with me!

Michael   Why always the act!

Dada   Nothing wrong with me. I reared a family –

Michael   And look at us now!

Dada   Reared – family – reared – that could –

Michael   Don't you know fathers don't have to gam on to their children the great men they are?

Dada   Made men of ye! – Proud! – Reared a family –

Michael   Honest to God, Dada, I tried to love you. What do you want to keep this up for?

Dada   Hah-haa, he loves me! Loves his old man!

Michael   Even though I saw through everything you did.

Dada   Hah-haa! He sees all! Loves me!

Michael   The big talk! What you were going to do!

Dada   Never – afraid – shadow!

Michael   How tough you are. Were. I never saw anyone carried away from you.

Dada (*viciously*)   Yeh-yeh-yeh! But you know nothing! But you know nothing!

Michael   And the big-shot friends –

Dada   You know nothing about it! Nothing about life!

Michael   Anthony Heneghan and the doctors. And I heard them myself laughing at you. And they still are.

Dada   Yaa – Yaa – Yaa – Yaa!

Michael   And you talk about pride! And you smoking cigars and drinking brandy with them and your wife on her knees scrubbing their floors.

Dada   Yaa – Yaa – Yaa – Yaa!

Michael   Where's your pride, Dada?

Dada   Don't – Don't talk irreverence about your mother, boy!

Michael   There's still nothing wrong with that?

Dada   D'ye hear him? What he's saying about your mother, boys? D'ye hear him! Now you hear this.

Michael   Is it a speech?

Dada   Now you hear this.

Michael   Sing 'I Hear You Calling Me'.

Dada   Now you hear this –

Michael   You were always heard – braying!

Dada Now you hear this – Now you hear this! Now you listen to me – You listen to me and I'll tell you a thing or two. Now you listen when I talk . . . Now, I want you all to hear, 'cause I have something to tell everyone . . . I'll tell you about life . . . I'll tell you all right about it . . . I'll . . . I'm going to . . . I have something to tell you all . . . I . . . I . . . Boys . . . Ah-haa! . . . Ah-haa! . . . And . . . (**Betty** *is heard coming downstairs. She enters dressed in overcoat and carrying a suitcase.*) Aha, the stranger, back to save the mouse, Ignatius! Desmond! Ah-haa, Hubert! Hubert!

Betty Are you coming with me or are you staying with them?

Harry Don't leave us, Mikey.

Hugo Don't leave us, Mikey.

Des Hit her, Mikey.

Dada Ah-haa!

Des Think of the children, Mikey.

Michael, *bewildered, looking almost stupidly at her. He looks at* **Des**.

Betty Don't look at him. He's the nice young brother you told me about.

Dada Ah-haa, Desmond!

Des Who do you think you're talking to!

Betty Are you coming? Now.

Des Who, Bitchey, do you think you're talking to? Watch it now. (**Betty** *exits, taking her suitcase.* **Harry**, **Dada**, **Iggy** *and* **Hugo** *follow her to the front door to cheer her departure.* **Michael**'s *hand on* **Des**'s *shoulder, restraining* **Des**.) Bitchey! Polly! English trash! Whore! (**Des** *becomes conscious of* **Michael**. *His first reaction is shame. He half-turns away; then he swings back.*) What are you looking at? What are you looking at me like that for?

Michael and **Des** *are in tears – or at the point of tears. The others rush back to the room.* **Dada** *gets up on the chair.*

Harry   Quickly – quickly – quickly! Something happening here with the two geniuses.

Hugo   They can't wait to see who's World Champ Carney.

Hugo   Don't come that game with me now.

Dada   What's he saying to you, Desmond?

Des   Nothing. Just looking at me. As if I was dirt.

Harry   What you doing about it? Talkin'?

Des   Everyone seems to think I'm a bit of a fool around here tonight.

Michael *makes a move to leave the room.*

Dada   Are you letting him go?

Harry   I don't think Des is no good.

Des *pulls* **Michael** *back.*

Dada	Ah-haa! Up to him, Desmond! Show him, Desmond!
Hugo	The cow's thump, Des!
Dada	For the honour of the Carneys!
Harry	I don't think Des is no good!
Dada	Ah-haa, the sneerer!
Hugo	The old one-two! Come on!
Iggy	Get it over with!
Harry	Des is no good!
Hugo	Aw, the cow's thump!
Iggy	Hit him!
Dada	Hit him! Hit him! Hit him! (*Like a schoolboy,* **Des** *hits* **Michael** *on the shoulder.*) Yaa-hah-haa! Man, Desmond Muck and trash! Again! Again! Keep it going!

Des *hits* **Michael** *again, this time more squarely.*

Des   The mouse! Couldn't command a woman even! A flea even!

Dada   Into it! Go on! Dirt! Dirt! Filth! Dirt! Muck and trash! Scum! Tinkers! Filth! (**Des** *knocks* **Michael** *with his next blow.*) Mister intelligent sneerer! We'll get them! Looking down their noses! On – on – on!

The others are cheering. **Des** *is pushed at* **Michael** *again.* **Michael** *throws him back.*

Michael   Jesus, our victory over *them*! (*Grabs a bottle.*) Are ye happy now? (**Des** *is coming at him again.*) Look at him: another victory for us over *them*! You don't know how to live either. (*He hits* **Des** *on the head with the bottle.* **Des** *falls and is still. Silence.*) . . . Is he all right? . . . see . . . Des? (*Examines* **Des**.) . . . Des? He's dead. (*Pause.*)

Iggy   What do we do now? Dada?

Dada   . . . Wha'? . . . Wha'? . . . Well . . . I mean . . . the chair.

Harry   What?

Dada   I was up on the . . . Ye were . . . Ye were all . . .

Harry   Who's ye?

Dada   I was up – Ye were all . . . Wha'? . . . I had nothing to do with – Not my fault . . . No, listen, boys. Him! Michael. Look at him. What kind of nature is in him? (**Harry** *turns away from* **Dada** *and joins* **Michael** *beside* **Des**'*s body.*) Always the cause of trouble in the house. Right from the beginning. The disrupter. (**Iggy** *joins* **Michael** *and* **Harry**.) Ignatius. Look at him. The disrupter, Hubert. (**Hugo** *joins* **Harry**, **Iggy** *and* **Michael**. **Dada** *is isolated in a corner of the stage.*) Hubert . . . Wha'? . . . Boys . . . Ye're not blaming me . . . No control over it. No one has any more . . . Did my best. Ye don't know how hard it is. Life. Made men of ye. What else could I have done? Tell me, Proud. Wha'? A man must have – And times were hard. Never got the chances. Not there for us.

Had the ability. Yas. And lost the job in the guards, police.
Brought up family, proper. Properly. No man can do more
than best. I tried. Must have some kind of pride. Wha'? I
tried, I did my best . . . I tried, I did my best . . . Tried
. . . Did my best . . . I tried . . .

The curtain falls slowly through the speech.

For a complete catalogue of Methuen Drama titles
write to:

Methuen Drama
36 Soho Square
London
W1D 3QY

or you can visit our website at:

www.methuendrama.com